LIVING

AS A YOUNG MAN OF GOD

KEN RAWSON

AN 8-WEEK CURRICULUM FOR MIDDLE SCHOOL GUYS

FOR AGES 11-14

ZONDERVAN®

ZONDERVAN.com/
AUTHORTRACKER
follow your favorite authors

**youth
specialties**

youth
specialties

Living as a Young Man of God
Copyright 2008 by Ken Rawson

Youth Specialties resources, 300 S. Pierce St., El Cajon, CA 92020 are published by Zondervan, 5300 Patterson Ave. SE, Grand Rapids, MI 49530.

ISBN 978-0-310-27879-5

Cover design by Toolbox Studios
Interior design by Mark Novelli, IMAGO MEDIA

Printed in the United States of America

10 11 12 13 • 20 19 18 17 16 15 14 13 12 11 10 9 8 7 6 5 4 3

For Noah Riley—may you become and live as a man of God. I love you, son.

ACKNOWLEDGMENTS

I attended my first Youth Specialties national resource seminar during my freshman year of college, in the spring of 1995 in Springfield, Missouri, where Doug Fields was the presenter. From that first day of training I was hooked on Youth Specialties (YS) and had a silly dream I might one day be a YS author.

Had it not been for my sweet wife, Jen, I'd still be dreaming that dream. Her incredible series for middle school girls (*Becoming a Young Woman of God* and *Living as a Young Woman of God*) paved the way for my dream to become reality. Her constant love, encouragement, grace, stubbornness, and belief in me have shaped my relationship with God and are making me a better man, husband, father, and friend. I love you, Jennifer Dawn.

Thank you to my dad, Larry Stilgebouer, who is a living demonstration of God's faithfulness and has given me a Christ-like model of what it means to be a father and a husband. Thanks also to my other dad, Ron Harris, for helping me draw near to what it means to be a godly husband and dad.

Thanks to all of the youth coaches from Central Christian Church, San Jose, California, who believed in me when I was just a chubby, loud-mouthed, mohawked, skateboarding middle schooler—Doug and Renee Daggett, Ted and Karen Goddard, Lon and Carla Hansen, Tony and Delaine Catudal, Pete and Jean Fong, Don and Debbie Ferguson, Scott and Erica Serface, Trey Hinkle, Kim and Nancy Robbie, Danny Quezada, Sean Mixon, and the rest of the congregation who never gave up on me.

Thank you to my three youth ministers, Steve Spray, Joel Brown, and Jim Coddington, who each shaped important parts of my story. Thanks to David Mullins, Pat Sehl, Jim Smith, and Trevor Hinz, who shared so much of their lives with me and will always be my band of brothers. Your lives and teachings are woven throughout these pages.

Thank you to Les Christie for your constant encouragement and my connection to home when you're out in the Midwest. Thanks to Phil Weece for believing one day I would write, and thanks to Kirk Longhofer for helping fine-tune my writing and communication. Thanks to Steve "Jake" Jacobs for being a constant reminder of God's grace and serving as my own little slice of Mike Yaconelli.

Thank you to First United Methodist Church in Wichita, Kansas, for allowing me to serve alongside a great staff as I minister to middle school students and their families.

Thanks to Sean Meade for showing me how to go for my dreams and to Kurt Johnston for helping me make middle school ministry simpler and for encouraging Jen to publish her book.

Thanks to everyone at Youth Specialties and Zondervan who had a part in putting this together. You guys are incredible!

Lastly, thank you to Ciera, Noah, and Charis, who went without lots of wrestling, swimming, playing, and karaoke singing while I finished this project. You've taught me so much about what it means to be a man and a dad, and I love you very, very much.

CONTENTS

INTRODUCTION: THE PUZZLE OF MANHOOD

Before the first tuft of hair escapes from the sweaty armpit of an 11-year-old boy, he's already confused about what it means for him to be a man. Throughout their brief early-adolescent years (11-14), boys are given different puzzle pieces, each one inscribed with information about the meaning of being a man.

Some pieces are from their fathers. Other pieces are from other adults, friends, and especially the media. In the end, our middle school boys sit at a metaphorical card table with a bad leg, attempting to put all these pieces together without the real picture on the box top to guide them.

Often their picture of real manhood looks this way:

Real men are tough athletes and fast runners, have six-pack abs, can bench-press at the very least their own weight, hit home runs, score touchdowns, have a bunch of girlfriends, climb rocks without harnesses, ride choppers, have cool cars, marry a trophy wife, end up with successful jobs making lots of money, and retire independently wealthy.

Then they're given a tattered baggie of worn-out puzzle pieces related to what Christian men are—that they're wishy-washy, go to church every day and evening, carry their Bibles with them everywhere, never even look at females, wear ties and pocket protectors, drive minivans, and stay at home the rest of the time.

This can't be what God had in mind.

Exactly! It's not.

And that's where *Living as a Young Man of God* comes into play. It consists of eight sessions dealing with feelings, girls, friends, and dads—and much more. Each session focuses on Jesus as our ultimate model of what it means to live as a young man of God. (Oh yeah—and it's also the "Part 2" of the first book in this series, *Becoming a Young Man of God*. It's a great idea to go through *Becoming* before you start *Living*, if you know what I mean.)

Before you jump in, briefly go over each element of the sessions. Also read the three tips to make the most of this resource.

SESSION ELEMENTS

At the beginning of each session **The Big Idea, Main Text**, and **What's the Point?** give the main Bible passage for the week and a brief overview of the focus of what you're teaching that week.

YOU'LL NEED

This list shows everything you might need to teach the session—depending on which of the many options you choose for various session sections. In other words, you may not need *everything* listed; skim through the chapter to find the options you like and make sure you have the supplies for those. In addition to what's listed, you'll nearly always need Bibles, pens, and copies of the reproducible pages at the end of the chapter.

RECAP SOUL WORK

See **Soul Work** explanation later in the introduction.

OPENING ACTIVITY

Here you're given some options for introducing the week's session to your guys. These activities are fun ways to get your students focused on where you're headed.

The Big Picture

This is the main point you're trying to get across. This is easily the most focused time of your teaching. Each session has an **Outline** sheet for the guys to follow for the **Big Picture**. If you're short on time, you might use your version of the **Outline**—the **Outline (Leader Guide)**—as your main lesson and pick and choose from the other options to fine-tune your time together. You'll find the **Outline (Leader Guide)** at the end of each chapter with the other reproducible handouts. It includes everything on the guys' sheet with some suggestions in parentheses to help you explain the ideas.

Breakdown

This is where you flesh out the idea presented in the **Big Picture** and give your guys time to wrestle with it.

Closing Activity

This section gives your guys real-world applications for what you just taught them—something practical they can do in response to what they learned—or take-home reminders.

Soul Work

At the end of each session, you'll give your guys a short take-home assignment called **Soul Work** that'll whet their appetites for the next week's session. You can also begin each week with a review of the previous week's Soul Work, using the section called **Recap Soul Work**.

THREE TIPS TO HELP YOU MAKE THE MOST OF *LIVING AS A YOUNG MAN OF GOD*

1. Make It Yours

There are a lot of options for each of the sessions—more than you'll probably have time for. Go through each chapter and use what will best connect with your students. Add your own stories and show appropriate transparency. Don't force the lessons. Tweak them and make them fit your group of guys, your context. If all you have is 10 minutes, use the **Outline** and the **Big Picture** section. If you want to show video clips every week, do that.

2. Have Fun

My guys connect better and pay more attention when I marry the lesson with having fun. Use some of the games to introduce your session. Tell funny or embarrassing stories from when you were their age. Eleven- to 14-year-old guys need appropriate outlets to diffuse their energy and help them process. Use the different options in the chapters to help direct some of that energy and help the guys stay connected.

3. Take a Week Off

Every four weeks I schedule a "week off" from teaching my guys. We'll do three weeks of Bible study or session study in small groups, and then take one week off. For this week off I still meet with my guys, but we go out and do something together—play video games, minigolf, hang out at the park, race go-carts, or go out to eat.

THANK YOU

Before you jump into this resource, I want to thank you for making a difference in the lives of your guys. Your notes, e-mails, phone calls, and the time you spend before and after teaching are shaping their souls and character.

I pray as you finish this resource, your guys will develop an unparalleled sense of trust, vulnerability, and love for each other in your group. I also pray they'll become godly young men—which in turn will not only radically transform their home life, but will also help them someday become better husbands and fathers who'll share the love of Christ with their children and grandchildren.

Lastly, I pray you'll be able to use this resource as a reliable "box top" in helping your guys put together all the pieces in the "puzzle of manhood." (At the very least you can use the book to prop up that bad table leg!)

CHAPTER ONE

BREAKING THE CODE: THE BEGINNING OF LIVING AS A GODLY GUY

THE BIG IDEA

Choose to become a godly guy.

Main Text

> "But the LORD said to Samuel, 'Do not consider his appearance or his height, for I have rejected him. The LORD does not look at the things human beings look at. People look at the outward appearance, but the LORD looks at the heart.'"
> (1 Samuel 16:7)

What's the Point?

We'll discuss "the boy code" and the inadequacies of how our culture views men. We'll talk about our biblical identity and our model (Jesus) and challenge the guys to seek confidence through developing responsible behavior, practicing spiritual disciplines, and being active in ministry.

Note: Those who've gone through the first book, *Becoming a Young Man of God,* will notice this chapter is similar in some ways to the first chapter of *Becoming.* That's on purpose. We want to make sure the points about going against the grain of cultural manliness and the boy code are reinforced as you transition into *Living as a Young Man of God.*

OPENING ACTIVITY
Option One: Who Would You Rather Be?

Welcome your guys and tell them that today you'll be talking about what it means to be a real man. Introduce this topic by having them "vote with their feet." This'll be fun, get them moving, and help them start thinking about the topic.

Explain that you're going to read a list of choices, and they'll have to pick one option or the other by moving to one side of the room. For example, you could say, If you were in a crowded elevator, would you rather make a really loud belch or a really smelly belch? If they choose loud, they'd go to the wall on the left; if they choose smelly, then they'd go to the wall on the right.

Here's the list of choices:

▷ fat or skinny

▷ computer programmer or body builder

▷ cry with your friends or cry by yourself

▷ car or motorcycle

▷ truck or minivan

▷ mustache or goatee

▷ bald or mullet

▷ glasses or contacts

▷ play football or play tennis

▷ be really smart or have huge muscles

▷ throw a perfect spiral or solve complex problems

▷ athlete or doctor

▷ Bill Gates or Arnold Schwarzenegger

Once your guys have stopped doing their Mr. Olympia poses, have them take their seats and ask them some of these questions:

▷ **What do you think it means to be a really manly man?**

▷ **If you were to make a list of the top-three things every guy needs to do or be to make him a real man, what would those things be?**

YOU'LL NEED

Your favorite manly DVD (if you don't have a favorite, rent some wrestling video or some kind of action movie starring a burly dude); pencils, crayons, markers, paper, and any other art supplies you think the guys could use (pipe cleaners, play dough, etc.); a Halloween mask, a winter ski mask, some athletic mask, etc., or supplies to make a mask; an oversized sweatshirt or sweatshirts and lots of duct tape to make a homemade straitjacket(s); an inexpensive key for each one of your guys; a dark-colored marker

USE LIFE STORIES

Jesus taught in stories. Whenever you can, share your own stories with your guys. These are just a few kinds of stories I like to use with my guys:

• *Funny Stories:* Anytime I can use a story to make my guys laugh, I'm connecting with them. Whether it's a dumb joke or a story that makes me look like an idiot, kids love funny stories. More important, guys connect with these stories.

• *Failure Stories:* Share about the times when you blew it. Times when you got in trouble with your parents, when you were self-centered and it cost you a relationship, or when you blew a great opportunity are great teaching tools. Failure stories help your guys see you as a real person instead of some glorious ideal they'll never reach.

CONTINUED >>

▷ **When you watch TV or movies, how are really manly guys portrayed? What are their personalities? What kinds of things do they do?** *(Possible answers: Think athletes, news reporters, action heroes, superheroes...none of them are fat or ugly, etc.)*

Briefly share from your life about what you thought it meant to be manly when you were a middle school guy. Maybe it meant being strong, having a girlfriend, cussing, or simply having a wispy moustache. Whatever it was, talk about what you thought made a manly man.

Transition to the **Big Picture** by saying something like, **What most people think it means to be a real man isn't true at all. Being a real man isn't about how strong you are, how fast you run, the kind of car you drive, the money you make, how pretty your girlfriend is, or any other lame measurement of manliness. Today we'll talk about what it really means to be a man.**

Figure out who has the next birthday and have him open up your time in prayer, asking God to show all of you what being men is really about.

Option Two: Manly Clip

As you begin, ask your guys what some of their favorite action movies or TV shows are. After they're done sharing, tell them you brought along one of your favorite guy movies, and you'd like to show them a clip.

Watch the brief clip, then ask your guys these questions:

▷ **In this clip how would you describe the hero?** *(smart, strong, brave, etc.)*

▷ **How do action movies usually portray guys? In other words, what kind of guys are usually the heroes? What are they like?**

▷ **How would you describe the ultimate action hero? If you had to make an action movie, what would your hero be like—how would he look; what would he do for a job; what would he drive, etc.?**

▷ **Let's switch from movies to the real world. What do you think it takes to be a real man? How's a man supposed to act? What makes a guy manly?**

Briefly share from your life about what you thought it meant to be manly when you were a middle school guy. Maybe it meant being strong, having a girlfriend, cussing, or simply having a wispy moustache. Whatever it was, talk about what you thought made a manly man.

Transition to the **Big Picture** by saying something like, **What most people think it means to be a real man isn't true at all. Being a real man isn't about how strong you are, how fast you run, the kind of car you drive, the money you make, how pretty your girlfriend is, or any other lame measurement of manliness. Today we'll talk about what it really means to be a man.**

Figure out who has the next birthday and have him open up your time in prayer, asking God to show all of you what being men is really about.

Option Three: Art Time

Have all your art stuff set out on the table before the guys arrive so you can jump into the topic without having to mess around with passing stuff out.

Some of your guys aren't going to connect best with a game or a movie. Engaging these guys' creative senses is your hook. This option is great because it gives you insight into what the guys really think.

Tell your guys today you're going to talk about what it means to be a manly man. But first you want to know what *they* think it means to be manly. Instruct each student to create what he thinks is a very manly guy. Give the guys five minutes to create their masterpieces and then have each one share about his manly creation.

Point out the features that make their creations manly, such as athleticism, money, muscles, girls, etc. Use their own creations to talk about the things most of us look at as indicators of manliness.

Briefly share from your life about what you thought it meant to be manly when you were a middle school guy. Maybe it meant being strong, having a girlfriend, cussing, or simply having a wispy moustache. Whatever it was, talk about what you thought made a manly man.

Transition to the **Big Picture** by saying something like, **What most people think it means to be a real man isn't true at all. Being a real man isn't about how strong you are, how fast you run, the kind of car you drive, the money you make, how pretty your girlfriend is, or any other lame measurement of manliness. Today we'll talk about what it really means to be a man.**

• *War Stories:* Share stories from your teenage years. Anytime you can share what it was like to sit in class, walk down the hall, see that cute girl, take a pop quiz, or have a bad teacher or a good teacher, you'll connect with your kids. Anything you bring up from your days as a teenager will resonate with and communicate to your boys.

Figure out who has the next birthday and have him open up your time in prayer, asking God to show all of you what being men is really about.

THE BIG PICTURE

Abstract Alert: What you're about to share with your guys in this section is really abstract, and they may need your help spelling it out. Be patient with them and try to make sure all your guys are on board. These ideas are so important to understand and will be referred to often.

Option One: The Mask We Wear

Share with your guys that before you talk about what it means to be a man, you first have to talk about the biggest lie about guys: The mask.

Put on the mask you chose or made and ask some of these questions (try to solicit some of the answers given, if possible):

▷ **Why are masks fun?** *(You can pretend to be someone you aren't, try out different personalities.)*

▷ **What do masks do?** *(They hide who you really are.)*

▷ **What kinds of masks are made to protect you?** *(Catcher's mask, fencing mask, face mask in football, etc.)*

Next find some way, in your own words, to say the following: **We all wear one mask I want to talk with you about. You can't see this mask, but just like the ones we just talked about, it prevents others from seeing your real face—it hides who you really are. And we use it to protect ourselves ALL the time.**

Go on, **It's the mask that says, "Everything's just fine," even when it's not. Most of us hide how we're feeling in some way or other. We don't tell people when we're sad, hurt, lonely, or scared.**

Next say, **Think of times when someone has asked you, "How are you?" How did you respond? What did you say—even if you were really sad or angry or disappointed? I can almost guarantee you said something like, "I'm fine." Or, "Everything's okay." We live with the idea that if we share our feelings, we're somehow less manly. We're weak. Wimps.**

Make sure your guys understand this idea and recognize times when they've hidden behind the mask you just described.

It may be easier for them to articulate this if you first share from your own life about times when you were a middle schooler or even times as an adult when you've hidden behind the mask. Share about a time when you were hurt, sad, or lonely and chose to hide behind the mask instead of sharing your feelings. Then ask them to share times when they've hidden behind the mask as well.

Transition to the **Breakdown** by saying something like, **The mask is part of "the code."[1] Guys have a code saying guys must act and think in certain ways. And if a guy doesn't, he must not be a real man. However, as we'll see next, the code is NOT our model for being real men.**

Option Two: Make Your Own Straitjacket

Ask your guys if they know what a straitjacket is. If they don't, explain what one is and then ask if anyone would like to wear one.

Now if you've been working any time at all with middle school boys, the thought has crossed your mind to put them in straitjackets (but for other reasons). Nevertheless, you'll need to decide if you want to pick just one volunteer to put on your homemade straitjacket or if you want to put it on each guy.

Whichever you choose, have the student who'll wear the straitjacket sit in a chair and put the large sweatshirt on. Then wrap him in enough duct tape to constrict his movement and keep him from getting out of it. (And no, you may not keep him in it for the rest of the night.)

Once your victim(s)...er, student(s) is under wraps and has tried to escape, ask him some of the following questions:

▷ How do you feel? What's it like to be stuck?

▷ How long do you think you could stay in this straitjacket? Could you stay in it forever?

▷ What are the benefits of being in a straitjacket?

▷ What's the worst part about being stuck this way?

[1] William Pollack does an amazing job of describing masks and the boy code in his book *Real Boys: Rescuing Our Sons from the Myths of Boyhood*. New York: Random House, 1998. It's a great resource about the world of boys becoming men.

Let your student(s) out of the straitjacket(s) and then find some way, in your own words, to say the following: **I want to talk with you about another kind of straitjacket we all wear. You can't see it. The straitjacket is part of "the code," the idea that to be a real man, a guy must act and think in certain ways. And if you don't, then you must be a wimp.**

Continue, **However, this code is a straitjacket. You become stuck having to fit this mold, this idea about what a man is. And it constricts you. It keeps you from being who God made you to be because you're so worried about appearing weak.**

Make sure your guys understand this idea and recognize times when they've felt forced into acting, thinking, or doing something just because not doing so would have made them appear less manly.

It may be easier for them to articulate this if you first share from your life about when you were a middle schooler (or even an adult), and you felt as if you were forced into the straitjacket of manliness—doing something daring, using inappropriate humor, being tough, etc. Then have the guys share times when they felt they had to do something manly to fit the code.

Transition to the **Breakdown** by saying something like, **We've all felt the power of the code. We've all felt as if we needed to fit some kind of idea of what it means to be real men and avoid anything that would make someone think we're less than men. However, as we'll see next, the code is NOT our model for being real men.**

Option Three: Tough Questions

With options one and two being more abstract, you might find it easier to walk the guys through some of these questions:

▷ **When was the last time you felt hurt, lonely, afraid, sad, or scared?** (With this being such a deep and personal question, especially with guys, you won't get any worthwhile answers until you share from your life about the last time you felt this way.)

▷ **When you've been hurt, lonely, sad, afraid, etc., have you ever pretended everything was just fine even when it wasn't?**

▷ **When someone has asked you how you're doing, did you ever lie and say something like, "Everything's fine," even when it wasn't?**

▷ Why do you think guys are afraid to share their feelings?

▷ Have you ever done something really manly? What kinds of manly things have you done?

▷ What are some other measurements of manliness?

▷ When have you ever felt ashamed or embarrassed because you either couldn't or didn't want to do something manly?

▷ Some things are clearly not considered okay for guys to do—play with dolls, practice ballet, sew, excel in school, be awkward in sports, etc. Can you think of any other ones?

▷ How do you feel about these guy-approved lists?

Transition to the **Breakdown** by saying something like, **Unfortunately, guys have this "code" we follow. The code is the idea that a guy must act and think in certain ways and only do certain things. And if you don't do these things, then you must be a wimp. However, as we'll see next, the code is NOT our model for being real men.**

BREAKDOWN

This section is really about the meat of the issue. You've established with your guys that our culture's view of what it means to be a real man is unrealistic. You've shared with them about the code and how a guy is considered manly as long as he keeps the code. But that isn't our model, either.

In a sense, in some small way, I hope your guys begin to notice "the emperor isn't wearing any clothes"—this belief they hold so strongly is full of holes. If this culture's definition of being a real man is untrue or lacking, what does it mean to be a real man? That's what you're breaking down.

Go through the **Outline** and have your guys read the Scriptures and fill in the blanks. After you've finished the **Outline**, transition to the **Closing Activity** by saying something simple such as, **Since we know now what it means to be a real man, we're ready for our last step.**

CLOSING ACTIVITY

Option One: Pick One

Bring some real-life application to your time together by having each one of your guys pick one of the three actions under number three on the **Outline** (being responsible, having a relationship with God, or serving others) to work on this week. Say something like, **Before we leave tonight, I want you to take another step toward being a man.**

Then have the guys do two things. Have each draw a circle around the option he's going to try this week and then write down exactly what he's going to do and when he's going to do it, right below his choice. (For example, a student could circle "has a relationship with God" and write, "I'm going to read four psalms this week and journal about them.")

You may need to give your guys some practical ideas for things they can do this week to show responsibility, develop a relationship with God, or serve someone. Next go around and have each guy share about what he wrote.

After everyone has shared who wants to, pass out this week's **Soul Work** sheet. Briefly go over it and answer any questions. Then have the person closest to you close your time together in prayer.

Option Two: Hand Out Keys

As you close your time together, reiterate to your guys how broken the code is and how they need to keep from getting locked up in it. Yes, this is a pretty abstract thought, but they should be able to get it, especially when you do the next part.

Hand each guy a key and tell him it's his to keep. He can carry it in his pocket, put it on his key ring, or string it around his neck—whatever he wants to do as long as it'll help him remember the point you're trying to make. The big idea is, this key will serve as a reminder that Jesus unlocks the code. (You may want to do something special to the keys so they stand out—that way your guys are less likely to forget them.)

Pass out this week's **Soul Work** sheet. Briefly go over it and answer any questions. Then have the person closest to you close your time together in prayer.

Option Three: Marker Fun

As your time comes to an end, remind your guys that the code isn't our model and Jesus breaks the code. Read 1 Samuel 16:7 to them again and talk about how God looks at the hearts of men, not their outward appearance.

Then grab your marker and write 1 SAMUEL 16:7 on the backs of the guys' hands (yeah, both of them) as reminders about what God looks at.

Pass out this week's **Soul Work** sheet. Briefly go over it and answer any questions. Then have the person closest to you close your time together in prayer.

BREAKING THE CODE: THE BEGINNING OF LIVING AS A GODLY GUY

1. The code isn't our <u>model</u>.

   "But the LORD said to Samuel, 'Do not consider his appearance or his height, for I have rejected him. The LORD does not look at the things human beings look at. People look at the outward appearance, but the LORD looks at the heart.'" (1 Samuel 16:7)

   (We just talked about this. The code says if you're a guy, you have to do certain things, act in certain ways. But God sees through the code. This verse says he looks at our hearts. He made us and loves us and has given us a real model for being a man...Jesus.)

2. <u>Jesus</u> unlocks the code.

   "People of Israel, listen to this: Jesus of Nazareth was a man accredited by God to you by miracles, wonders and signs, which God did among you through him, as you yourselves know." (Acts 2:22)

   (Jesus was accredited—or recognized, certified, qualified—by God. He was amazing! He was both fully God and fully man at the same time. There's never been anyone like Jesus. He's our model for what it means to be a real man.)

3. A real man is someone who—

   A. is <u>responsible</u>.

   "His master replied, 'Well done, good and faithful servant! You have been faithful with a few things; I will put you in charge of many things. Come and share your master's happiness!'" (Matthew 25:21)

   (A boy becomes a man when others are able to hold him responsible for things, when people can trust him to do what he says he'll do. God clearly rewards responsible people.)

   B. has a <u>relationship</u> with God.

   "...train yourself to be godly. For physical training is of some value, but godliness has value for all things, holding promise for both the present life and the life to come." (1 Timothy 4:7-8)

(A baby becomes a child when he can begin to eat regular food. You wouldn't give a baby a steak. Similarly, a boy becomes a man when he doesn't rely on his parents' faith but finds and builds a personal relationship with God on his own. Spiritual disciplines help us to experience a relationship with God in a deeper and more profound way.)

C. <u>serves</u> others.

"For we are God's handiwork, created in Christ Jesus to do good works, which God prepared in advance for us to do." (Ephesians 2:10)

(Lastly, a boy becomes a man when he thinks of other people before himself. When he decides to do ministry, serve God, or help with the church, he moves closer and closer to becoming a real man.)

BREAKING THE CODE: THE BEGINNING OF LIVING AS A GODLY GUY

1. The code isn't our _____.

   "But the LORD said to Samuel, 'Do not consider his appearance or his height, for I have rejected him. The LORD does not look at the things human beings look at. People look at the outward appearance, but the LORD looks at the heart.'" (1 Samuel 16:7)

2. _____ unlocks the code.

   "People of Israel, listen to this: Jesus of Nazareth was a man accredited by God to you by miracles, wonders and signs, which God did among you through him, as you yourselves know." (Acts 2:22)

3. A real man is someone who—

   A. is r_____.

   "His master replied, 'Well done, good and faithful servant! You have been faithful with a few things; I will put you in charge of many things. Come and share your master's happiness!'" (Matthew 25:21)

   B. has a _____ with God.

   "...train yourself to be godly. For physical training is of some value, but godliness has value for all things, holding promise for both the present life and the life to come." (1 Timothy 4:7-8)

   C. s_____ others.

   "For we are God's handiwork, created in Christ Jesus to do good works, which God prepared in advance for us to do." (Ephesians 2:10)

SOUL WORK

Can you imagine Jesus on a milk carton? No, not really. When I was a boy, missing and abducted children's photos could be found on the side of half-gallon milk cartons. At some point when Jesus was 12, he got lost, but he hadn't been kidnapped.

Check it out in Luke 2:41-52. Then answer these questions.

1. How often did Jesus' parents go to Jerusalem?

2. How long was Jesus missing?

3. When they found Jesus, what was he doing?

    (I'm guessing this isn't the whole story. I think the author, Luke, left out something about Jesus being grounded for the rest of his natural-born life or something....)

4. Have you ever gotten lost?

5. How did you feel?

6. How did you think Jesus felt when he realized his parents were gone?

7. So...Jesus was a total kid. He even ditched his parents. Sound like anyone familiar? That's right; Jesus used to be a middle schooler, too! Yet check this out: Hebrews 4:14-16.

Jesus was your age once. He had chores; he had annoying little siblings; he didn't always communicate well with his parents—yet he didn't do what?

_____ _____ _____ ← You can write your answer there.

Talk about a model we can live our lives after!

CHAPTER TWO

THE REAL MAN: JESUS AS OUR MODEL

THE BIG IDEA

Jesus was a real man.

Main Text

> "Jesus...has been tempted in every way, just as we are—yet he did not sin." (Hebrews 4:14-15)

What's the Point?

In this session we'll reinforce Jesus as the ultimate man. We'll take a quick look at him as a boy and give a strong case for his humanity and how he has experienced life just as we have, as a man growing up and grown-up. One thing separates him from us, though: He was without sin, which makes him the best model of a man we can follow.

RECAP SOUL WORK

Last week's **Soul Work** had to do with Jesus ditching his parents to hang out in the temple. The main idea was to get your guys thinking of Jesus as a middle schooler.

Ask them, **So what do you think Jesus was like when he was between 10 and 13?**

After you get some answers, ask if anyone answered the final question, which was based on Hebrews 4:14-16. The answer: He never sinned. Give a prize to any of your guys who attempted to answer the question and tell them today you're going to look at more about Jesus' personality.

OPENING ACTIVITY

Abstract Alert: Some of the **Opening Activity** options are really fun, but be patient with your guys in their thinking time. If they're quiet during your questions, most likely their brains are processing the information, and they might need your help.

They'll be switching from a very concrete game to something really abstract. It'll be good. You may just have to be patient.

Option One: LEGO Maniac Attack

Get two of your guys to volunteer for a competition and have them sit down at a table. Tell them this will be a timed contest, and the winner gets a valuable prize.

Once they're situated, give these instructions: **You'll each receive a box of some sort with instructions. Follow them exactly. The first one to build the creation correctly wins. Ready? Set? GO!**

Hand them each one of the duplicate boxes of LEGOs and watch the madness unfold. Once you have a winner, give both LEGO boxes to the volunteers and lead the group through these questions:

▷ **How would this competition have gone if neither one of you had the instructions or a model to follow?**

▷ **Why is it so important to have a model to follow with LEGOs?**

▷ **Just as you follow a set of instructions or a model to build something with LEGOs, we all kind of have models we follow to be men. Who or what are your models to follow as you become a man? Who or what are you getting instructions from on how to be a man?** (This is a hard, hard question. You may need to prompt them with who your model was for being a man when you were in middle school. For some things it might've been your dad. For other things it might've been guys on TV or in movies.)

▷ **None of our models is perfect. What are some ways your model has actually taught you how NOT to be a man or what a man shouldn't be?** (I know, I know, another tough question.)

YOU'LL NEED

Some prizes; two identical LEGO® boxes of the $5-7 sort, the small LEGO creations that take about five minutes to build—they're the super-econo versions, usually cars of some sort; the collage from *Becoming a Young Man of God,* if you still have it, or appropriate pages from man-focused magazines, glue, and a piece of paper or poster board to make another collage; a chair, preferably a broken one (if not, a regular one will do just fine); BYOBOL: bring your own baggie of LEGOs to give away, one per guy; a dark-colored marker

DISCUSSION TIP

Don't be afraid of silence. Let them think through these questions and restate the questions in as many ways and as many times as you feel necessary to prime the pumps.

If you can't afford to buy
two new boxes of LEGOs,
you have some other
options:

1. Borrow some LEGOs
and make a simple
creation. Then bring two
sets of the same pieces
you used to make your
example and have the
guys try to duplicate what
you made.

2. Have the guys draw
from a picture you've
brought. Then relate the
questions to the picture as
a model of what to draw.

3. Use play dough to make
a creation and have the
guys try to duplicate what
you created.

Transition to the **Big Picture** with this thought: **None of our models is perfect because no perfect people exist. But one man lived life just like you and had to become a man as well. Today we're going to talk about how Jesus is the one perfect man and our best model to teach us how to be real men.**

Have the person on your left pray for your guys and then head into the **Big Picture**.

Option Two: Super Logo Challenge

If you're the enterprising type, search the Internet for the logos or emblems that these 10 superheroes wear on their chests: 1. Batman, 2. Captain America, 3. Flash Gordon, 4. The Fantastic Four, 5. The Green Lantern, 6. Iron Man, 7. Robin, 8. Spider-Man, 9. Superman, 10. Mr. Incredible.

Then create a handout displaying each of the logos along with the names—the object is to have your guys guess what logos go with what superhero names.

You'll probably have more than one winner, so toss out your prizes and then ask these questions:

▷ **Who is or was your favorite superhero?**

▷ **Is there a guy in your life who you really look up to? Maybe he's not a superhero, but you kind of look up to him and want to be like him.** *(My example: I didn't have a dad. But I looked up to my brother. A ton.)*

▷ **What makes this guy so great? Why do you think he's worth imitating?** Or you might ask, **What's the one best thing about this guy you hope to make part of your personality?** *(My example: He was so funny and strong, and girls loved him. He could do wheelies on his motorcycle, and he took me on rides with it. He was totally cool.)*

▷ **Every superhero has a weakness. What are some weaknesses the guy you look up to has? What makes you think, "This guy is great, but I still don't want to be this way"?** *(My example: My brother has a temper. When he's angry, I can't even talk to him.)*

Once they're all done saying, "I don't know…" and you've shared (if you shared), say something like, **No matter who you look up to, no one's perfect. And as you become a man, you look for other men to imitate, to act like. Everyone does it. Today we're going to talk about THE man, the one guy who has no weaknesses. He's our best example of what it means to be a real man: Jesus.**

Have the guy on your left open up in prayer and then move to the **Big Picture**.

Option Three (A): Collage from *Becoming*

In *Becoming a Young Man of God* we spent some time talking about the idea of our culture's view of what men should be and have—for example, handsome and lots of muscles, with a nice car, many girlfriends, lots of money, etc. If you still have the collage from last time, get it out and ask the following questions:

▷ **Remember back when some of us made this collage? What was the point of it? What were we trying to get at?** (If your guys are struggling a bit with verbalizing what it's all about, gently nudge them along.)

▷ **Has anything changed? What does our culture think a real man is?**

▷ **In what ways does our culture give us a bad model to follow for what a real man is?**

Then say something like, **Our culture believes if you're a man, then you have to be strong, do crazy acts of bravery, have lots of girlfriends, be able to fight anyone, have no fear, and know everything. Except no one does or has all those things—and not all of those things are good anyway. As we'll see, we really only have one man to follow, one man who's a perfect example of what a real man is: Jesus.**

Have the guy on your left open in prayer and then go to the **Big Picture**.

Option Three (B): No Collage from Last Time?

If you don't have a collage, you can make one easily enough. Just cut some appropriate pages from magazines such as *Men's Health, ESPN The Magazine, Rolling Stone,* etc.

You can either have the guys make a collage themselves (which will take the bulk of your time), or you can just slap one together on your own and use it as an example of the point you're trying to get across. Either way, you'll do all right, and they'll get the idea.

If you're reading this on the way to church or don't want to do a collage, just bring in a couple of magazines and thumb through them, pointing out the photos that illustrate the absurdity of our culture's ideal man.

Whether you have the collage or just a few magazines, point out to the guys how the media communicates to them what a real man is. Help them understand how our culture thinks men should be winners, tough, smooth-skinned, strong, handsome, muscular, etc.

Once you feel they're getting the idea, ask them this question: **According to our photos, what do our culture and the media say a real man is?**

After you get some answers, say something like, **Our culture believes if you're a man, then you have to be strong, do crazy acts of bravery, have lots of girlfriends, be able to fight anyone, have no fear, and know everything. Except no one does or has all those things—and not all of those things are good anyway. As we'll see, we really only have one man to follow, one man who's a perfect example of what a real man is: Jesus.**

Have the person on your left open in prayer and then go to the **Big Picture.**

THE BIG PICTURE

From the **Big Picture** you want your guys to walk away with the idea that Jesus is the ultimate man. He felt the same things they do and experienced the very same struggles they have now and will go through in the future. The main idea you want them to come away with is: They can trust Jesus as the ultimate model of manhood.

Play the game "Sit down if...." The game is easy. Have everyone stand and have them answer by sitting down if they answer yes to any statement (and then stand up again before you say the next one). You can make up your own or use the short list I made. Whichever you choose, make sure to use the very last statement on my list.

Sit down if...

...you've ever flown in a plane.

...you've ever made a cape and worn it around the house.

...you like cheese.

...you've ever met someone famous.

...you've blamed your burp on someone else.

...you've never read a book of the Bible.

...you've ever fallen asleep in church.

...you've ever met Jesus face to face.

Ask them all to sit down and then remind them, **One of the best ways to meet Jesus "face to face" and to discover him is through reading the Bible.**

Which is what you're going to do next...except instead of reading through the whole Bible, right now you'll be giving them the shorthand version of the kind of guy Jesus was. Rip through your **Outline**.

Once you're done with the **Outline**, move to the **Breakdown** with something like, **Jesus was a REAL man. He wasn't a fairy-tale or made-up person. He's not a character. He was fully God and fully man. And he lived a human life just as we do. Even though the Bible doesn't exactly say so, we can probably assume Jesus had crushes on girls, skinned his knees, hit his thumb with a hammer, and maybe could even burp the Hebrew alphabet.**

Continue, **Because Jesus was a man—a perfect man, who never sinned—we can trust him as our model for what it means to be a real man.**

BREAKDOWN
Option One: Jesus Haiku

I'm a sucker for haiku, and it's a great way for kids to have fun and process what they're learning.

THAT'S A LOT OF BIBLE!

The verse list on the Outline isn't exhaustive. However, my fear is that if I spend too much time with each point, I'll just bore the kids to tears. So you'll want to balance how much time you spend on each point.

When I teach, I tear through the list so the guys are writing and listening, and then I spend a lot of time on the last point: Jesus is the model to follow.

Tell your guys they're going to write haiku. A haiku is a short Japanese poem traditionally about nature, although it can be about anything. A haiku has five syllables in the first line, seven syllables in the second line, and five more in the last line.

Give them this example:

Middle school guys rule.

They are becoming real men.

They make me feel proud.

After they understand what a haiku is (and they've quite likely written haiku at school), pass out paper and pens and instruct them to write haiku about what they just learned. After they ask what they just learned, remind them about the idea that because Jesus was human like us but never sinned, we can trust him as our model for becoming men.

Give them a few minutes to come up with their best haikus. After they've finished, have each guy share his own creations and give all of them lots of encouragement. Consider making your own haiku to share with them as well.

Tell your guys they did a great job and head on to the **Closing Activity.**

Option Two: The Director's Chair Improv Game

Use this fun game to get your guys to make the connection about Jesus being a great model to follow in becoming a man.

Of course, you may have to introduce the idea of improv, which is drama "as you go," all made up on the spur of the moment. There aren't any scripts to memorize; you just wing it.

Here's the setup: You're the director of a great movie being filmed about life as a middle schooler. Use the scenarios given. Have different guys try out the different roles and have fun.

The first scene will always be a middle schooler in some type of situation. After the guys do their brief improv, you yell out like a director, **Aaaaaaaand cut!** Then say, **This time I want you (the person playing the middle school student) to be Jesus as a middle schooler. Take it from the top. (Which means start over again.)** You can read these scenes to the guys, write them on cards or paper, whatever works for you.

▷ Scene One: The Kitchen Table

The players: Middle School Mike (later Jesus) and Mom

The scene: Middle School Mike is getting ready for school when his mom yells at him about why he didn't take out the trash last night as he was told. Already frustrated because he couldn't find a clean shirt to wear, Mike answers his mom....

▷ Scene Two: Lunch at School

The players: Middle School Mike (later Jesus) and the New Kid

The scene: It's lunchtime at school, and The New Kid is at Mike's table. He's really quiet, as most new kids are. Mike's just hanging out with his buds, but they're all kind of wondering about the New Kid. All of a sudden, the New Kid opens his mouth and asks a question....

▷ Scene Three: At the Movies

The players: Middle School Mike (later Jesus) and his best friend John

The scene: John's mom drops the boys off at the movies. Mike thought they were going to see a certain movie and play video games. John wants to go to an R-rated movie. The plan is to buy the tix for the movie they were originally going to see but just go to the other movie. Mike feels unsure about this. He says...

After the performances, ask the guys a couple of these questions:

▷ **Why does it seem silly to try to act how Jesus would act?** *(Possible answer: A lot of times it's because he seems too perfect. Unrealistic.)*

▷ **Why is it so hard in real life to act the way Jesus would act? Or do the things he would do? Or respond as or say the kinds of things he would?** *(Because we think of ourselves first. We want what we want, when we want it, and how we want it.)*

▷ **How does the fact that Jesus was able to do the right thing encourage you?** *(If he could do it, I know I can, with God's help.)*

Move to the **Closing Activity** by saying something to the tune of, **Because Jesus was human like us, we can look to him as the ultimate model of what it means to be a man.**

Option Three: Object Lesson

Place your broken chair in front of your guys and run through some of these tough questions. Remember—some of your guys will find this tough, so be patient, don't be afraid of silence, and walk them through the concepts. When they connect, it'll be worth your time.

▷ **What do you guys see?** *(Uhh...I know the answer is Jesus but it looks like a chair to me....)*

▷ **If you could pick any chair in this room, why wouldn't this chair be your first pick?** *(Because it's broken.)*

▷ **If you were going to build a chair, why would you not want to use this one as your model?** *(Because the next chair I make would break the same way. It's not a good chair. I'd need to make a better one.)*

▷ **Earlier we talked about our models for manliness and the guys many of us look up to as models of how we'd like to be as men. Some might look up to someone rich such as Bill Gates. Others might look up to famous athletes or even their own dads. How are these guys like broken chairs?** *(Jesus is the absolute perfect model. While these others guys might know how to make money, play sports, or even be good fathers, they still aren't the best models for becoming real men.)*

Here are two other ways you can relate the broken chair to broken models of manhood. You don't have to use both of these or either of these. But do use some kind of transition to help your guys see Jesus as the man they want to model their lives after. Again the statements are really abstract, but they'll help hammer home our theme.

▷ **If you sit in a broken chair, you might possibly get hurt. When we use imperfect men as our models, we sometimes can get hurt, too (because of unrealistic expectations of manhood, etc.).**

▷ **Sometimes you don't know a chair is broken before you sit in it. In the same way be careful who you pick as a model for what it means to be a man. In some way he's broken.**

Move to the **Closing Activity** by saying something to the tune of, **Because Jesus was perfect, we can look to him as the ultimate model for being a man.**

CLOSING ACTIVITY

Option One: LEGO Giveaway

To help your guys remember Jesus is the ultimate model to follow, hand each of them one LEGO to keep in his pocket this week. Every time the guys feel their LEGOs, we want them to remember who the perfect model is.

Pass out this week's **Soul Work** sheet and have everyone form a circle. Pray they'll remember this week to trust Jesus as the model for being a real man.

Option Two: Write Out a Prayer

Pass out copies of the **Prayer** handout and have your guys write simple prayers to God asking him to help them trust Jesus and look to Jesus as the true model of manhood.

Have the guys take their prayers home. Tell each one to tape his prayer in a place where he'll see it so he can say the prayer every day this week.

Then pass out this week's **Soul Work** sheet and stand together in a circle. Pray they'll remember this week to trust Jesus as the model for being a real man.

Option Three: More Marker Fun

If you didn't use the marker idea from last week, this could be a good closer for you. Use a dark marker and write on the back of one of each of your guys' hands: HE'S THE MAN.

Tell the guys to use the note as a reminder this week. Every time they look down at their hands or someone asks them what the note means, they can remember Jesus is the ultimate man they can model their lives after.

Then pass out this week's **Soul Work** sheet and stand together in a circle.

Pray they'll remember this week to trust Jesus as the model for being a real man.

THE REAL MAN: JESUS AS OUR MODEL

1. Jesus...

"...has been tempted in every way, just as we are—yet he did not sin." (Hebrews 4:15)

(A lot of times we think of Jesus as more of a fairy-tale man than a real man. He just seems too perfect and very unreal. However, Jesus was human just as we are.)

...was a <u>teenager</u>.

"And as Jesus grew up, he increased in wisdom and in favor with God and people." (Luke 2:52)

...got <u>frustrated</u> with his mom.

"'Woman, why do you involve me?' Jesus replied. 'My hour has not yet come.'" (John 2:4)

...didn't always <u>get along</u> with his brothers.

"Even his own brothers did not believe in him." (John 7:5)

...got <u>mad</u>.

"So he made a whip out of cords, and drove all from the temple courts, both sheep and cattle; he scattered the coins of the money changers and overturned their tables. To those who sold doves he said, 'Get these out of here! Stop turning my Father's house into a market!'" (John 2:15-16)

...felt <u>happy</u>.

"Jesus said, 'Let the little children come to me, and do not hinder them, for the kingdom of heaven belongs to such as these.'" (Matthew 19:14)

...was <u>tempted</u> to do bad things.

"Then Jesus was led by the Spirit into the wilderness to be tempted by the devil." (Matthew 4:1)

...was <u>brave</u>.

"A furious squall came up, and the waves broke over the boat, so that it was nearly swamped...He got up, rebuked the wind and said to the waves, 'Quiet! Be still!' Then the wind died down and it was completely calm." (Mark 4:37, 39)

...felt <u>lonely</u>.

"About that time Jesus shouted...'My God, my God, why have you deserted me?'" (Matthew 27:46, CEV)

...was <u>scared</u>.

"Going a little farther, he fell with his face to the ground and prayed, 'My Father, if it is possible, may this cup be taken from me. Yet not as I will, but as you will.'" (Matthew 26:39)

...was so <u>sad he cried</u>.

"Jesus wept." (John 11:35)

2. Jesus wasn't a <u>super-man</u>. He was the ultimate <u>real</u> man.

"The Word [Jesus] became flesh and made his dwelling among us. We have seen his glory, the glory of the one and only [Son], who came from the Father, full of grace and truth." (John 1:14)

OUTLINE

THE REAL MAN: JESUS AS OUR MODEL

1. Jesus...

"...has been tempted in every way, just as we are—yet he did not sin." (Hebrews 4:15)

...was a _____.

"And as Jesus grew up, he increased in wisdom and in favor with God and people." (Luke 2:52)

...got _____ with his mom.

"'Woman, why do you involve me?' Jesus replied. 'My hour has not yet come.'" (John 2:4)

...didn't always _____ with his brothers.

"Even his own brothers did not believe in him." (John 7:5)

...got _____.

"So he made a whip out of cords, and drove all from the temple courts, both sheep and cattle; he scattered the coins of the money changers and overturned their tables. To those who sold doves he said, 'Get these out of here!

Stop turning my Father's house into a market!'" (John 2:15-16)

...felt _____.

"Jesus said, 'Let the little children come to me, and do not hinder them, for the kingdom of heaven belongs to such as these.'" (Matthew 19:14)

...was _____ to do bad things.

"Then Jesus was led by the Spirit into the wilderness to be tempted by the devil." (Matthew 4:1)

...was _____.

"A furious squall came up, and the waves broke over the boat, so that it was nearly swamped...He got up, rebuked the wind and said to the waves, 'Quiet! Be still!' Then the wind died down and it was completely calm." (Mark 4:37, 39)

...felt _____.

"About that time Jesus shouted...'My God, my God, why have you deserted me?'" (Matthew 27:46, CEV)

...was _____.

"Going a little farther, he fell with his face to the ground and prayed, 'My Father, if it is possible, may this cup be taken from me. Yet not as I will, but as you will.'" (Matthew 26:39)...was so

_____.

"Jesus wept." (John 11:35)

2. Jesus wasn't a

_____.

He was the ultimate

_____ man.

"The Word [Jesus] became flesh and made his dwelling among us. We have seen his glory, the glory of the one and only [Son], who came from the Father, full of grace and truth." (John 1:14)

PRAYER

My prayer for this week:

Because you love me.

Amen

"Don't be a baby!"

"Stop crying!"

"Don't be a wimp!"

"Be tough!"

"Be a man!"

You've probably had adults say (or yell) some of these phrases to you. You know the feeling when you can't hold it in anymore. Things are bad. You're hurting. You want to cry. But you can't let it out. You can't. You haven't cried in a long, long time. And you're not about to now. Because "big boys don't cry."

1. How long has it been since you last cried?

2. What made you so sad?

3. Why aren't boys allowed to cry?

4. What do you think is the one feeling boys are allowed and even encouraged to feel?

5. Read John 11:1-36 and fill in the blank.

   Jesus wept because he _____ Lazarus.

6. How does that make you feel?

   E-mail, write, or call a man you respect this week and ask him these three questions:

7. Why do people think it's weak if men cry?

8. Were you allowed to show your feelings when you were my age?

9. What would you say to someone who keeps his feelings bottled up and secret?

CHAPTER THREE

FEELINGS, PART ONE: AM I A WIMP? WHAT ARE THESE FEELINGS?

THE BIG IDEA

Real men don't hide what they're feeling.

Main Text

> "Sadness is good for the heart. That's why sorrow is better than laughter. Those who are wise are found where there is sorrow. But foolish people are found where there is pleasure." (Ecclesiastes 7:3-4, NIrV)

What's the Point?

Guys aren't allowed to cry. But sadness isn't the only feeling men have a difficult time processing. In this session we'll give guys permission to feel and help them learn how to discuss those feelings without fear or awkwardness. We'll show them Jesus was incredibly sensitive and compassionate.

Special Note: This session gets very close to the heart of the boy code, the idea that "Everything's just fine." Boys tend to mask their feelings. They're conditioned from early on to hide their feelings. They're told not to cry. They need to be tough.

Unfortunately, this creates a suppression of feelings and pain, which can only continue for so long before it explodes, usually in anger.

I'm asking you, man to man, to share honestly and openly about your own struggles with feelings throughout this session. Your stories and careful transparency will make or break this time together.

Share about how you grew up and in what ways you weren't allowed to feel. Talk about how you still deal with this. If you grew up in a healthy family where you were encouraged to share your feelings, please share about how this helped you.

More than anything, share your stories.

RECAP SOUL WORK

This session is so packed, you won't want to spend a ton of your time recapping the **Soul Work.** However, let the guys take a few swings at the answer for the last question. The correct answer is Jesus wept because he loved Lazarus.

Also have them share the answers they received to the three questions they were to ask older males.

Congratulate those who did their **Soul Work** and give them some kind of prize. Then jump into this week's session.

OPENING ACTIVITY

Option One: *Pleasantville*[2]

Introduce this idea of feelings by asking your guys to do the following things:

▷ **Raise your right leg if you felt great this week.**

▷ **Lift your left arm if you felt really mad.**

▷ **Stand up if you felt stressed out.**

▷ **Sit down if you felt sad this week.**

▷ **Pretend you're sleeping if you felt tired this week.**

Tell your guys to wake up, then say something like, **Can you imagine living in a place where no one felt anything except "nice" all day long, every day? What would that be like?**

[2] Fields, Doug, and Eddie James. *Videos That Teach 2*. Grand Rapids, MI: Zondervan, 2002.

Next set up the movie's story and play the clip (start clip at 01:42:17, "Bud Parker William Johnson"; stop at 01:46:40, "And you can't stop something that's inside you").

Then ask some of these questions:

▷ **If you had a choice, which world would you choose—black-and-white (perfect but flat and no feelings) or colorful (exciting but painful sometimes)? Why?**

▷ **What emotions—good or bad—do you keep inside because expressing them isn't considered very manly?**

▷ **Why aren't guys encouraged to express their feelings?**

▷ **When was the last time you had to pretend everything was okay because you didn't feel safe sharing how you were really feeling?**

▷ **Have you ever come to this youth group and put on a mask? Have you been here when you were sad but pretended everything was okay?**

After sharing, move toward the **Big Picture** by saying something like, **Today we're going to talk about what to do with your feelings.** Then have someone pray for the group as you explore this issue of feelings.

Option Two: Group Charades

As you probably know, charades involve someone trying to get a group to guess a word or phrase by acting out whatever the word or phrase is without talking. With group charades, the game is the same, only the roles are reversed. So the group acts out the word or phrase together, and one person has to guess it.

Today's category will be feelings. You'll want to write each feeling on a piece of paper or card with big lettering so you can show it to the group without your guesser seeing it. You can have one person guess all the items or trade off. Whatever you do, ask for a volunteer who wants to have fun.

Here are the feelings the person will need to guess:

▷ ANGRY

▷ HAPPY

▷ SAD

- ▷ IN LOVE
- ▷ EXCITED
- ▷ BORED
- ▷ SCARED
- ▷ CONSTIPATED

After your guys are finished, ask them some of the following questions:

- ▷ **Which feelings** are **really easy for you to express?**
- ▷ **Which feelings are really hard to show?**
- ▷ **Why aren't most guys encouraged to display their emotions?**
- ▷ **When was the last time you had to pretend everything was okay because you didn't feel safe sharing how you were really feeling?**
- ▷ **Have you ever come to youth group and put on a mask? Have you been here when you were sad but pretended everything was okay?**

After sharing, move toward the **Big Picture** by saying something like, **Today we're going to talk about what to do with all these feelings.** Then have someone pray for the group as you explore this weird world of feelings.

Option Three: Emotionally Evocative Images

If you already have a copy of Youth Specialties' *Every Picture Tells a Story*[3], this is a great use for it. If you don't have it, you'll want to pick up a copy for all the different ways you can use it. It's a really effective resource—and not just for this particular group exercise.

It's one thing to talk about feelings. It's another whole deal to help your guys experience feelings, which is the purpose of this option.

[3] Oestreicher, Mark. Grand Rapids, MI: Zondervan, 2002

Introduce this option by saying something like, **Today we're talking about feelings. But instead of simply talking about them, I thought we'd take some time to actually feel them.**

Pass around or show the emotion-evoking pictures and have your guys spend some time looking at the photos. Encourage the guys to think about what's going on in each picture. They don't need to rush through the stack.

After a set amount of time, use the following questions to help guide your discussion:

▷ **Which picture stood out to you the most and why?**

▷ **What was the most interesting picture?**

▷ **Which one was the saddest?**

▷ **Which picture is similar to how you've felt this week?**

▷ **Why is it so difficult to talk about feelings?**

▷ **Why aren't guys encouraged to share their feelings?**

▷ **When was the last time you had to pretend everything was okay because you didn't feel safe sharing how you were really feeling?**

▷ **Have you ever come to youth group and put on a mask? Have you been here when you were sad but pretended everything was okay?**

After sharing, move toward the **Big Picture** by saying something like, **Today we're going to talk about what to do with all these feelings.** Then have someone pray for the group as you explore this weird world of feelings.

THE BIG PICTURE

The **Big Picture** has three purposes:

1. Reintroduce the code and reiterate that it's false, bad, and completely unhelpful. If you say this enough times in many different ways, they'll be better able to connect with it and keep hold of it long term.

2. Help your guys see that Jesus had all kinds of feelings and didn't try to hide them. We've only listed five. Your summary will really be key.

3. Give the guys permission to allow themselves to feel and not try to hide their pain.

All your notes, including your transition to the **Breakdown**, are on the **Outline (Leader Guide)**.

Also, make a copy of the following note and post it where you can read it often.

Thanks again for taking the time to write notes to your guys, call them on the phone, and invest in their lives by teaching them a godly perspective on manhood.

Your guys may frustrate you, and you may feel as if you aren't getting enough of your sessions through to them, but, brother, you are making a VERY REAL difference in the lives of these students.

Be patient. The fruit of your labor, especially with middle school guys, takes time.

BREAKDOWN

Option One: "You Probably Shouldn't..."

We've established the idea that our guys should be real men and not hide their feelings, which is good. The harder part is helping the guys learn, now that they don't hide their feelings, what they're supposed to do with the feelings.

This worksheet goes over five situations similar to the ones listed on the **Outline**, the five Jesus went through. This will help your guys know different things they can do with their feelings instead of hiding them. Hand out the worksheets and either let your guys go through them on their own or do it together.

After they've finished, go over the answers (1. E, K; 2. I, C; 3. J, F; 4. A, L; 5. D, H). Let the guys share stories—in fact, encourage it. For some of the guys, this may be the first time they've shared any painful stories. Be sensitive not to let one or two of your more extroverted students monopolize the sharing.

When your guys are done talking about feelings, head on to the **Closing Activity**.

Option Two: "The Mud Flats"[4]

Some guys may mask their feelings and pain by escaping through other means—even addictive behaviors, such as drinking, smoking, etc. While this is a normal reaction, the consequences of their choices can be devastating, either now or later.

Share this story with your guys:

> **Just outside Anchorage, Alaska, there's a place called the Turn-Again Arms. This particular area has one of the fastest tide rates in the world. The tide rushes in and out at about 10 feet per minute. The water is so cold that if you got caught in it, you'd die within a few moments.**
>
> **When the tide is out, there's a huge flat area of mud. It looks like a great place to ride off-road vehicles. But this area—called the mud flats— is not just mud but also glacial silt. When the tide rushes out, the leftover water settles quickly, leaving air pockets, which form vacuums.**
>
> **You never know where the vacuums are, and they're never in the same place twice. If you step in one of them, it will suck you in, and you can't get out. It's not exactly like quicksand but more like superglue as it locks you in.**
>
> **In the summer of 1991 a couple who'd just gotten married decided to spend their honeymoon in this part of Alaska. They went out riding ATVs and decided to ride around on one particular mud flat.**
>
> **The bride's vehicle stalled, and she jumped off to see what the problem was. She jumped into one of these areas of glacial silt and sank in up**

[4] Rice, Wayne. *Hot Illustrations for Youth Talks* on CD-ROM Version 1.0. Grand Rapids, MI: Zondervan, 2001.

to her knees. As she struggled to get out, she sunk in to her thighs. Her husband rode up on his ATV, and she warned him not to get off his vehicle.

People on the road above them saw what was happening and called for help, yelling at the man not to get off his vehicle. Within moments the fire department arrived and tried to blast the bride out of the mud flat using water hoses.

It didn't work. Then they brought in an army helicopter from an Air Force base. They tried to pull her out with a rope and harness attached around her waist. As the helicopter pulled up her legs dislocated. They knew if they pulled any more, they would've ripped her legs from her body.

They tried to put a wet suit around her, thinking that when the tides came in, it would keep her warm. But they could only get the wet suit around part of her body. When the tides came in, she died while her husband helplessly watched.

Transition to the **Closing Activity** by saying, **This tragic, true story illustrates what it's like when we try to hide and escape our feelings.** Explain, **The alternatives all look so good. So inviting. You see people enjoying these things, and you just want to get out there and have fun. But instead they suck you in and ultimately take your life. All those escapes will do is trap you and take away everything meaningful in your life. Don't hide or try to escape through some type of high. Deal with your feelings head-on and ask for help.**

Continue to the **Closing Activity**.

Option Three: Case Study

Here's one more way you can help your guys process what to do with their feelings. Read this case study out loud or pass out the **Kirk's Blog** handout and allow the guys time to read it.

> **Great news today. My dad is leaving my mom. I guess last night's fight was the last one. I knew something was up when I found them sitting on the couch after I got home from school. My mom looked as if she was going to die. My dad says he and my mom aren't getting along. No doubt. And he's moving out, and they're getting divorced, and I need to think about who I want to live with.**
>
> **Nice. Real nice. So I've pretty much been playing video games all day. I have to finish up a report, but I could honestly care less. You guys are all I have now. I would love it if someone would call me.**

Next ask your guys to write a short response to Kirk as if they were commenting on his blog. What would they say to their friend?

After a time of sharing responses, ask some of these questions:

▷ **You guys did a great job responding to Kirk. Let's change this up a bit and focus on this guy. What did he do that was very good?** *(Possible answer: He shared his feelings. He didn't keep them bottled up.)*

▷ **What did he do that wasn't very good?** *(Played video games, ignored his homework.)*

▷ **What else can Kirk do to deal with his sadness?**

▷ **When he does go back to school, how can Kirk be real with his life and not pretend everything is okay? What advice would you give him to keep him from trying to hide behind the code?**

Move to the **Closing Activity** and affirm your guys' good responses by saying something like, **The number-one thing we have to remember is that hiding behind a mask and saying, "Everything's fine" only causes damage. We've got to be real.**

CLOSING ACTIVITY

Option One: Code Covenant

Make copies of the **Code Covenant** for each of your guys and read through it together. Encourage each guy to sign a covenant and tape it to his mirror or some other place where he can see it and read it every day. Don't forget to sign it as well and hand out this week's **Soul Work** sheet.

Stack all the covenants in a pile, have everyone place their hands on them, and close your time this week together praying for God's strength to live beyond the code. Give the guys their covenants back to take home before you leave.

Option Two: T10 Challenge

If you have a particularly tough-guy kind of group, help them remember Jesus was so manly that he didn't have to pretend not to be sad and have them take the T10 challenge.

Have the guys look at the **Outline** and circle John 11:35, which is, "Jesus wept." Congratulate them on memorizing a Bible verse.

The T10 challenge is for each guy to tell 10 different people what John 11:35 is this week. Have them write down the names of the people they tell the verse to on the back of their **Outlines** and bring the list with them next week for a cool prize.

Close your time together by passing out this week's **Soul Work** sheet and praying together that each time they recite John 11:35, they'll be reminded of how tough Jesus was and how he didn't hide behind the code.

Option Three: Four-Day Feeling Journal Challenge

Honestly, our guys feel so much every day. Middle school is a tough, tough time for them as they develop intellectually, spiritually, socially, and of course, physically. They have lots and lots of feelings going on, and it's no wonder they hide them. For some guys, especially those in denial of their feelings, it can be a real eye-opener when they journal just a few of the feelings they experience every day and the range of emotions they experience.

Pass out the **Four-Day Feeling Journal** handout and challenge and encourage the guys to write down how they're feeling throughout four different days next week. They don't need to write every single feeling they experience. If so, they'd be done by 7:30 a.m. Just have them write a few each day.

The point is to help the guys become more self-aware of the gamut of feelings they deal with every day. Go through the example and answer any questions they have.

After everyone gets what to do, pass out this week's **Soul Work** sheet and pray in a circle, asking something like, **God, help us all as we step out from behind our masks and stop pretending everything's always okay. Please give these young men wisdom in dealing with their feelings and being real. Amen.**

OUTLINE (LEADER GUIDE)

FEELINGS, PART ONE: AM I A WIMP? WHAT ARE THESE FEELINGS?

1. The <u>code</u>: "Everything's <u>fine</u>." Even when it's <u>not</u>.

   (The code: Guys have to be tough. They must hide their feelings.

   You may think this idea of a code is lame. However...if you get physically hurt, what do you do? If you get your feelings hurt, what do you do? Finish this phrase: Big boys don't _____? *What? Cry.)*

2. You can't hide your <u>pain</u> as well as you might think.

   (It comes out in anger, seclusion, taking risks, escapes, cutting, relationships, alcohol and other addictions, etc.)

3. Truth: *Real* men don't hide what they're <u>feeling</u>.
   A. Jesus felt <u>sad</u>.

      "Jesus wept." (John 11:35)

   B. Jesus felt <u>secluded</u>.

      "About that time Jesus shouted... 'My God, my God, why have you deserted me?'" (Matthew 27:46, CEV)

   C. Jesus felt <u>sincere love</u>.

      "Jesus looked at him and loved him." (Mark 10:21)

   D. Jesus felt <u>scared</u>.

      "Going a little farther, he fell with his face to the ground and prayed, 'My Father, if it is possible, may this cup be taken from me. Yet not as I will, but as you will.'" (Matthew 26:39)

   E. Jesus felt <u>sympathy</u>.

      "When Jesus landed and saw a large crowd, he had compassion on them, because they were like sheep without a shepherd." (Mark 6:34)

(You'll probably need to be specific that Jesus loved people with a deep love. The love in Mark 10:21 isn't meant in a sexual way. Jesus had a deep love for people, a love so amazing he died for us.)

4. If you want to be a real man, <u>let yourself feel.</u>

(Most of us have avoided painful and sad feelings so much we almost don't even feel them anymore. Pain and sadness are not enjoyable, so we try to escape those feelings by doing something else or trying to pretend they don't exist. You have permission to feel.

Jesus didn't try to tough it out. When he was sad, he cried. When he was scared and alone, he prayed for help. When he loved someone, he wasn't afraid to show it. When he saw people who needed help, he felt compassion for them instead of ignoring them.)

"Sadness is good for the heart. That's why sorrow is better than laughter. Those who are wise are found where there is sorrow. But foolish people are found where there is pleasure." (Ecclesiastes 7:3-4, NIrV)

(Those who are wise don't try to escape or hide their feelings. They know their feelings well and are able to help others through their pain instead of being helpless.

Share with your guys a specific way this has been true in your life. Talk about a time when you faced your feelings instead of drowning them in a pitcher of beer or hiding behind a mask of toughness or minimizing your feelings through humor.)

Move toward the **Breakdown** with something like this: **Now that you have permission to stop hiding your pain and a model to follow, let's talk about how to deal with those feelings.**

FEELINGS, PART ONE: AM I A WIMP? WHAT ARE THESE FEELINGS?

1. The c_____: "Everything's f_____." Even when it's _____.

2. You can't hide your _____ as well as you might think.

3. Truth: R_____ men don't hide what they're _____.

    A. Jesus felt s_____.

    "Jesus wept." (John 11:35)

    B. Jesus felt s_____.

    "About that time Jesus shouted...'My God, my God, why have you deserted me?'" (Matthew 27:46, CEV)

    C. Jesus felt s_____.

    "Jesus looked at him and loved him." (Mark 10:21)

    D. Jesus felt s_____.

    "Going a little farther, he fell with his face to the ground and prayed, 'My Father, if it is possible, may this cup be taken from me. Yet not as I will, but as you will.'" (Matthew 26:39)

    E. Jesus felt s_____.

    "When Jesus landed and saw a large crowd, he had compassion on them, because they were like sheep without a shepherd." (Mark 6:34)

4. If you want to be a real man, _____.

    "Sadness is good for the heart. That's why sorrow is better than laughter. Those who are wise are found where there is sorrow. But foolish people are found where there is pleasure." (Ecclesiastes 7:3-4, NIrV)

"YOU PROBABLY SHOULDN'T..."

Instructions: For each of the situations below pick two options from the "possible answers" list. You'll use each letter once.

For example: You probably shouldn't <u>G</u>. Instead you could <u>B</u>.

Possible Answers

A. Run to your room and shut the door. Then ask to live with your youth leader.

B. Begin with #1.

C. Tell your dad how alone you're feeling.

D. Say, "Go ahead and cry, you little baby!"

E. Bust up laughing.

F. Pray and ask God to help you be very alert, quick, and brave.

G. Burp and use this paper to wave the stink away.

H. Tell your friends to cut it out and go hang out with your unpopular friend.

I. Kidnap him and hold him hostage until his dad changes his mind.

J. Tell your teammate to suck it up and take it like a man.

K. Share with him about how you felt when your grandma passed away.

L. Be real and tell them how sad this is for you and how much it hurts.

1. Andy came to school after being gone all last week. He wouldn't even pick up his phone or return your texts or anything. When you asked what was up, he said his family's 16-year-old cat Elvis got run over, and he just hasn't felt like going to school or hanging out or anything.

   You probably shouldn't _____. Instead you could _____.

2. Jim's dad was just offered a new job, so his family's moving away. Jim is your best friend in the entire world. No one understands you like he does. This stinks.

   You probably shouldn't _____. Instead you could _____.

3. Your baseball team is finally playing Bill's team, and your friend Jeff is pitching. Unfortunately, Jeff's fastball just hit Jesse, the dude who bats in front of you, in the face. Jesse is down on the ground, and Jeff doesn't look sorry at all. You're next at bat.

   You probably shouldn't _____. Instead you could _____.

4. Your dad and mom just sat you down and told you they're getting separated. You'll have to pick who you want to live with.

   You probably shouldn't _____. Instead you could _____.

5. Bruce isn't a popular kid in school. In fact, the dude is weird. But he's been your friend forever. For some reason a couple of your friends who don't know Bruce are teasing him. Bruce looks pretty sad and is walking away.

   You probably shouldn't _____. Instead you could _____.

KIRK'S BLOG

Great news today. My dad is leaving my mom. I guess last night's fight was the last one. I knew something was up when I found them sitting on the couch after I got home from school. My mom looked as if she was going to die. My dad says he and my mom aren't getting along. No doubt. And he's moving out, and they're getting divorced, and I need to think about who I want to live with.

Nice. Real nice. So I've pretty much been playing video games all day. I have to finish up a report, but I could honestly care less. You guys are all I have now. I would love it if someone would call me.

What are you going to write to help Kirk deal with his pain?

CODE COVENANT

CODE COVENANT

I, _____, do hereby make a covenant between God, my youth group leader, and myself to fight the "boy code" starting today, _____ (today's date).

▷ I will not be ashamed of my feelings.

▷ I will ask for help when I'm feeling alone.

▷ I will not answer, "Everything's fine" when asked if I'm okay and I'm not.

▷ I will be wise and seek God through my sadness.

▷ I will not be embarrassed to love people sincerely.

▷ I will sympathize with others who are hurting.

"Sadness is good for the heart. That's why sorrow is better than laughter. Those who are wise are found where there is sorrow. But foolish people are found where there is pleasure." (Ecclesiastes 7:3-4, NIrV)

CODE COVENANT

I, _____, do hereby make a covenant between God, my youth group leader, and myself to fight the "boy code" starting today, _____ (today's date).

▷ I will not be ashamed of my feelings.

▷ I will ask for help when I'm feeling alone.

▷ I will not answer, "Everything's fine" when asked if I'm okay and I'm not.

▷ I will be wise and seek God through my sadness.

▷ I will not be embarrassed to love people sincerely.

▷ I will sympathize with others who are hurting.

"Sadness is good for the heart. That's why sorrow is better than laughter. Those who are wise are found where there is sorrow. But foolish people are found where there is pleasure." (Ecclesiastes 7:3-4, NIrV)

FOUR-DAY FEELINGS JOURNAL

You're going through so many changes and stresses in your life. Sometimes it's hard to deal with your feelings because so much is happening; it's hard even to know what you're feeling.

Take the **Four-Day Feelings Journal** challenge and write down throughout the day some of the different feelings you're having. You don't have to write a lot. I think you'll be surprised at how many different feelings you have each day. Journaling how you're feeling during the day can teach you tips and tricks about how to deal with the next day.

Date: May 8

I'M FEELING...	WHY...	THOUGHTS...
Tired	Just woke up	Mornings stink.
Angry	My sister is annoying.	Ignore her next time.
Stressed	Stupid pop quiz	Who needs to no speling?
Excited	Two words: *Cute girl*	Very nice...
Tired	School's done.	Time to play PSP
Tired	Practice went long.	Got to do report.
Stressed	Got to do report.	Uh, got to do report.
Angry	Lame sister	She's so annoying.
Superhappy	Cute girl just called.	I think I'm in love.

Date:

I'M FEELING...	WHY...	THOUGHTS...

Date:

I'M FEELING...	WHY...	THOUGHTS...

Date:

I'M FEELING...	WHY...	THOUGHTS...

Date:

I'M FEELING...	WHY...	THOUGHTS...

SOUL WORK

We guys may struggle with hiding most feelings, but when it comes to showing anger, we're professionals. Most of us have very short fuses, and it doesn't take much gasoline to blow up.

We aren't alone. Even Jesus got angry. Check it out! Read the verses listed and write down why Jesus got mad in each case.

1. Scripture: Why

    John 2:13-17   _____

    Mark 3:1-6   _____

    Mark 11:12-20   _____

2. The Bible also gives us a warning in Ephesians 4:26-27. Go read it. The writer of the book of Ephesians says never to give the devil a...what?

3. What do you think that means? (Ask an adult guy if you're not sure because you'll need it for the next question.) Hint: Whenever you climb trees or rocks, you need this for your toes to push you up to the next level.

From *Living as a Young Man of God* by Ken Rawson. Permission to reproduce this page granted only for use in buyer's youth group. Copyright ©2008 by Youth Specialties.

4. How has anger ever gotten a foothold on you? How has it led to other things, positive or negative?

5. Ask your dad or that adult male you respect to help you one more time: "What was the best advice you've ever gotten for dealing with anger?" Whatever the answer is, write it down and share it at our next meeting.

CHAPTER FOUR

FEELINGS, PART TWO: HOW TO DEAL WITH YOUR ANGER

THE BIG IDEA

Real men don't hide what they're feeling.

Main Text

> "My dear brothers and sisters, take note of this: Everyone should be quick to listen, slow to speak and slow to become angry, because our anger does not produce the righteousness that God desires." (James 1:19-20)

What's the Point?

The only acceptable feeling for guys to express seems to be anger. Our anger fuels our rage and aggressive instincts. It's no coincidence that most violent criminals are men. We'll talk about how guys need a way to deal with anger in healthy ways without being destructive. We'll also look at Jesus' righteous anger and how it compares to self-serving anger.

RECAP SOUL WORK

Last week's **Soul Work** introduced the guys to the idea of anger by having them read the passages of Scripture when Jesus is angry. The guys also explored Ephesians 4:26.

Ask your guys to share about times when anger got a foothold on them, leading them into something worse. Also have them share the advice they got when they asked guys in their lives about the best advice they've ever received on how to deal with anger.

Make sure to affirm the guys who are doing their **Soul Work** each week and continue to encourage the guys who just don't seem to get it done. Then lead into the **Opening Activity**.

OPENING ACTIVITY

Option One: *Happy Gilmore*

Remind your guys that last week you talked about feelings and how to deal with them. Tell the guys you want to show them a clip from a movie to introduce the feeling of anger you're going to talk about today.

No introduction about the scene is really necessary, unless you want to tell them how many times you've actually watched this movie.... Play the clip from *Happy Gilmore* (start clip at 00:22:45, "All right. Remember what I said, eh?"; stop when Chubbs frustratedly clubs his head).

Then ask your guys some of these questions:

▷ **Tell me about a time when you guys have felt angry that way?**

▷ **What kinds of things make you feel the angriest?**

▷ **Are you someone who gets angry really easily or someone who can take a lot before he gets mad?**

▷ **Have you ever seen someone so angry he was out of control?**

▷ **Have you ever been so angry you were out of control?**

▷ **When you get angry, do you burst out or do you get really quiet? Or do you deal with your anger in a different way?**

▷ **What's the best advice anyone's ever given you about how to deal with your anger?**

▷ **What advice would you give to a small group leader who's getting really angry at his guys dorking around? (Just kidding...)**

Affirm your guys for being open about their angry feelings. Then make this point: **Most guys have a hard time dealing with their feelings. A lot of us stuff them down until we can't stuff anymore, and then we explode in anger. Even when we're feeling other emotions, we'll often erupt in anger because it seems the only emotion**

YOU'LL NEED

Happy Gilmore, Black Sheep, or *Spider-Man 3* DVD; pieces of poster board or butcher paper, paintbrushes, and different colors of paint (or spray paint); *Tombstone* DVD; someone willing to share about his own struggle with anger and how he's learned to deal with it; lots and lots of eggs and somewhere to chuck them without hurting anything

GUYS NOT TALKING?

Your guys probably won't have any trouble talking about when they've felt angry or about which things upset them. However, when the questions start getting personal, they may begin getting quieter and quieter.

If this is the case, you may consider jumping to part of **Option Two**: Sharing your story.

CONTINUED >>

we know how to deal with. Today I'm going to give you some great help in dealing with your anger.

Have the oldest student pray for your time together and then jump into the **Big Picture.**

Backup Funny Illustration: *Black Sheep*[5]

If you can't get a copy of *Happy Gilmore* but still want a funny way of introducing the session via movie clip, you can use this scene from *Black Sheep* (start clip at 00:59:56, a car screeches to a stop; stop at 01:01:41, "Who'd you vote for?"). Then ask the same questions listed for *Happy Gilmore.*

Backup Action-Serious-Fantastic Illustration: *Spider-Man 3*

This is a great scene when Spider-Man talks to Venom and tries to help him understand the power of the alien suit (start clip at the battle between Venom and Spider-Man; stop after Venom says, "I like feeling angry!"). Then ask the same questions listed for *Happy Gilmore.*

Option Two: Your Story

Once again you probably have no better way of connecting with your guys than through sharing your own stories of dealing with anger.

Think about situations that made your blood boil when you were a middle schooler: Unreasonable or abusive parents, rude teachers, bullies at school, your siblings, etc. Also consider those times when you feel angry as an adult.

Introduce this topic of anger by sharing from your life. Say something like, **As we talk about anger, I want to be honest with you guys. This is something I was really bad at as a teenager and something I still struggle with sometimes.**

Make sure to include something about feeling your angriest when you're trying to tell a story and instead of listening, the people you're talking to are laughing, joking around, making burp noises...oh, I'm sorry, that's just my group of guys!

Anyway, get them more involved in this topic by asking some of the questions from **Option One**. If your guys are willing to open up and share, affirm them. Then tell them something like this: **Most guys have a hard time dealing with their feelings. I know I did. We stuff them down**

---

[5] Fields, Doug, and Eddie James. *Videos That Teach*. Grand Rapids, MI: Zondervan, 1999.

until we can't stuff anymore, and then we explode in anger. **Even when we're feeling other emotions, we'll erupt in anger because it seems the only feeling we know how to express. Today we're going to give you some great help in dealing with your anger.**

Have a student pray for your time together and then jump into the **Big Picture.**

Option Three: Graffiti

Introduce this feeling of anger by sharing a short story about a time when you felt angry as a middle schooler or some things that really upset you in school: Mean teachers, bullies, the girl who dumped you, etc. Then have your guys name some things that make them feel angry.

Next grab your paint, or spray paint if you're brave, and some butcher paper and paint or write all the different people, things, and stuff that made you feel angry when you were in middle school. (*Caution:* Make sure you don't spell out people's names—use the first letter of a person's first name instead; that way you can still express your feelings without "naming names" and potentially upsetting others. And make sure your guys follow your lead!) After you're finished, have your guys do likewise. Encourage students to pick colors to symbolize the anger they feel toward those people or things.

Talk through some of the things they wrote. Ask them to share any stories behind the words they wrote (again, make sure they don't name names!). Get them more involved by asking some of the questions from **Option One**.

If your guys are willing to open up and share, affirm them. Then tell them something to this effect: **Most guys have a hard time dealing with their feelings. I know I did. We stuff them down until we can't stuff anymore, and then we explode in anger. Even when we're feeling other emotions, we'll erupt in anger because it seems the only feeling we know how to express. Today we're going to give you some great help in dealing with your anger.**

Have the oldest student pray for your time together and then jump into the **Big Picture.**

BIG PICTURE

This **Outline** is a long one. It may be really tough for your guys to move through. I've really tried to make it easy. But this whole deal about anger is HUGE. Be patient. When you're done, they'll have some really good answers.

Online resources:

The statistics for violent crimes and arrests come from a study by the U.S. Department of Justice, found at these sites:

www.ojp.usdoj.gov/bjs/crimoff.htm

www.ojp.usdoj.gov/bjs/pub/ascii/wo.txt

Some of the tips for ways to deal with anger and when to ask for extra help can be found here:

www.kidshealth.org/teen/question/emotions/deal_with_anger.html

BREAKDOWN

Option One: *Tombstone*

Now that you've given your guys some good ideas on dealing with anger, let them see a really creative way of handling it.

This illustration has two parts. You have to stop the first clip immediately so you don't give away the answer. Make sure you preview this clip so you know exactly what you're looking for.

Introduce the movie clip from *Tombstone*, a Western starring Kurt Russell as Wyatt Earp and Val Kilmer as Doc Holliday. Both cowboys are near the ends of their careers. Wyatt is trying to settle down, and Doc is dying of tuberculosis. While trying to make money running a saloon, Doc runs into a little bit of trouble with an angry cowboy (start the clip at chapter 9, 00:35:35, "Johnny Ringo": "Thanks, Kate"; stop after the gunslinger puts his gun away, and the camera pans to the guy in the red shirt or the old guy with the beard, 00:39:15).

Then ask, **What do you think is going to happen next?**

After your guys have given their best answers, play the rest of the clip (stop the clip at 00:39:55 when Johnny Ringo smiles and walks away).

Next ask these questions:

▷ Instead of getting angry, what does Doc do to diffuse the situation?

▷ Does he come away looking okay to others even though he doesn't fight?

▷ What are some good choices you can make the next time you feel angry?

Move to the **Closing Activity** by saying something like, **Feeling angry isn't always a choice. But what you do with it can mean life or death.**

Option Two: Guest Speaker or Interview

Help this session hit home with your kids by having a guest speaker come in and share his struggles and answers to dealing with anger. Consider asking your minister to share about his or her own struggles with anger. Or maybe the minister can point you in the direction of someone in your congregation who'd be willing to share.

You can either have your guest share a story, or you can interview your guest. Make sure to ask your guest for permission, and if he's willing, have students ask him questions.

When your speaker is finished, say thank you and move to the **Closing Activity** by telling your guys you have one last challenge for them before you finish up.

Option Three: Righteous or Selfish?

Discerning whether anger is from selfish motives or righteous motives can be tough, particularly for a middle schooler.

Tell your guys you want to help them begin learning how to tell whether their anger is self-centered or righteous by giving them some different situations to figure out. Pass out copies of **Righteous or Selfish?** and have your guys take their best shots at deciding which kind of anger each situation represents.

When they're done, walk through each of the situations with them and talk about what makes anger righteous or selfish (answers—1. selfish, 2. righteous, 3. righteous, 4. selfish, 5. righteous, 6. could be either).

Transition to the **Closing Activity** by affirming how difficult it can be to know the source of your anger and encourage the guys by telling them they'll get better with practice.

CLOSING ACTIVITY

Option One: Pick One

By now you may be running out of time. Here's a quick way to wrap up your session and give your guys an action step to accomplish.

Challenge them again from Paul's words, this time in the book of Ephesians. This verse is the very last thing on the **Outline**: "Get rid of all bitterness, rage and anger, brawling and slander, along with every form of malice" (Ephesians 4:31).

Explain, **Paul told the first Christians to get rid of a bunch of the garbage holding them back. Things we talked about today: Anger and rage.**

Have your guys look at the bottom of the **Outline** and pick one of the ways to try to deal with their anger this week. Have the guys circle their choices, star them, do something to them so next time they're angry (you know, on the way home in the car with their moms asking, "What did you learn about tonight, honey?" "Nothing!"), they'll have one option to try.

Finally, hand out this week's **Soul Work** sheet and tell the group next week you'll be talking about girls. Pray for the guys, asking God to help them remember how to deal with their anger.

Option Two: Eggs Away

When talking about all this anger, you might notice some of your guys really struggling. Maybe they have issues of righteous and selfish anger, and they need a way to deal—now.

Tell your guys you're going to end this evening by going on a little field trip. Have them follow you out to a place you've designated outside. Now hand each guy an egg.

Then say something like, **In your hand is an egg. But I want you to do something that may seem weird. I want you to think about something you're really angry about. Maybe a person who has mistreated you or a situation you're angry about. I want you to think of the person or situation and put your anger on the egg, then I want you to throw the egg as hard and as far as you can.**

After your guys give you a look that says, "Are you serious? Are you sure this is okay? I'm not going to get grounded for this, right?" let 'em fly. Let your guys throw as many eggs as you have.

After you've explained to the neighbors or your pastor why eggs are on their cars (okay, bad joke—seriously, make sure the area you choose is far away from anything the boys could damage, etc.), take your guys back inside and ask them some of the following questions:

▷ **How do you feel?**

▷ **How did you feel when you were throwing your eggs?**

▷ **Has destroying your eggs done anything to fix your situation?**

▷ **In what ways do you feel less angry?**

▷ **What are some other physical things you could do to express your anger in a healthy way?**

Once everyone is done sharing, and parents are outside your door wondering why you guys aren't finished yet, hand out this week's **Soul Work** sheet.

Tell the guys next week you'll be talking about girls, then pray God will help them remember how to deal with their anger.

Option Three: Repent

Dealing with anger is tough. And some of your guys have dealt with it poorly. Partially because they didn't know any better, and partially because their selfish, sinful natures got ahead of them.

What they may need more than anything right now is silence between them and God so they can repent of how they've handled sin in the past—and pray for help in the future.

Remind them of what the apostle Paul wrote to the Christians in Ephesus: **"Get rid of all bitterness, rage and anger, brawling and slander, along with every form of malice" (Ephesians 4:31).**

Explain, **Paul knows our lives are filled with things holding us back from really experiencing the life God has for us. He challenges the Christians in Ephesus to get rid of all their rage and anger. And God's Word is challenging us to do this today as well.**

Then give the guys some time of silence and encourage them to ask for forgiveness. To repent. Tell them this time is between them and God to apologize for how they've mishandled their anger in the past, ask forgiveness, and ask for help in handling anger in the future.

After a time of silence pray for your guys out loud—for God to help them, this week and for the rest of their lives, to deal with their anger in healthy, nonviolent ways.

Before they leave, hand them this week's **Soul Work** sheet and tell them next week you'll be talking about girls.

OUTLINE (LEADER GUIDE)

FEELINGS, PART TWO: HOW TO DEAL WITH YOUR ANGER

"Do not be quickly provoked in your spirit, for anger resides in the lap of fools." (Ecclesiastes 7:9)

(Underline those last seven words: *Anger resides in the lap of fools.* God's Word says foolish people hold on to anger and keep it ready to use anytime. And according to the latest statistics, men are fools since our anger gets us into a lot of trouble.)

According to the U.S. Department of Justice, men account for <u>78</u> percent of all arrests. Men also commit <u>86</u> percent of violent crimes.

(Wow! That's a lot. Obviously guys have a real anger problem. So how can we deal with this problem? Here are four things you should know.)

1. Know what you're <u>feeling</u>.
   A. "Love...is not easily angered." (1 Corinthians 13:4-5)

   (The Bible says true love isn't easily angered. That's how we should be...not easily angered.

   Because we hide our feelings a lot and don't express them and haven't dealt with them in healthy ways before, many times what we think we're feeling is anger, but it's actually something else.

   What I mean is, we call something anger even when it's not only anger we're feeling but other emotions as well.)

   B. Instead of anger you may be feeling—
   ▷ <u>guilt</u> *(because you did something wrong or got caught).*
   ▷ <u>embarrassment</u> *(because of something unexpected).*
   ▷ <u>pride</u> *(because someone is putting you down).*
   ▷ <u>sadness</u> *(because of something said or done).*
   ▷ <u>pain</u> *(because you did something stupid).*
   ▷ some other feeling.

2. All anger isn't the <u>same</u>.

   A. Ask yourself: Am I angry because something wrong happened, or am I angry because I'm being <u>selfish</u>?

   (This is such an important distinction. Share a story here illustrating the difference. Here's what I mean:

   Situation: James asks if he can go out on Friday night. His parents tell him no because they have a family get-together to go to.

   If he's angry because he wants to go to the family get-together as much as he'd enjoy his armpit hair being pulled out one by one, then his anger is probably based on selfish reasons.

   If he's angry because he feels as if he wasn't given a choice, then it's probably an appropriate reason for anger.

   Dig deeper into this with the following:)

   B. Two kinds of anger: <u>Righteous</u> anger

   (Motivated by others, by bad things happening)

   (Righteous means "good, noble, fair, upright, just." This anger is caused because bad things happened or are happening to you or someone you care about through no fault of your own.

   Someone said or did something hurtful to you or a friend of yours. They gossiped about, ignored, or lied to you or a friend, etc. Or you're angry about some kind of injustice in the world, such as homelessness, war, a friend's parents' divorce, AIDS, etc.

   There are lots of right reasons for anger. Even Jesus got angry. Check it out:)

   "[Jesus] looked around at them in anger and, deeply distressed at their stubborn hearts, said to the man, 'Stretch out your hand.' He stretched it out, and his hand was completely restored." (Mark 3:5)

   (Here Jesus is ready to do something amazing—change someone's life forever. And all these people care about is Jesus breaking a law. [Note: Explain about the law he's breaking—no healing allowed on the Sabbath—so your guys have an idea why he's upset here.] In this moment, for these people, the law is more important than the person who's hurting. And Jesus is angry.)

C. Two kinds of anger: <u>Selfish</u> anger

(Selfishly motivated)

(This is the most common kind of anger. It's selfishly motivated because we aren't getting our way. We want something done our way, the way we do it, in our time.

For example, we could be:

▷ *angry at a person who takes too long in line.*

▷ *angry because our parents just said no to something we want.*

▷ *angry because people won't just leave us alone.*

Look at what Proverbs 29:11 says: "Fools give full vent to their rage, but the wise bring calm in the end." Sometimes being able to tell righteous anger apart from selfish anger can be really, really hard.)

3. Ways to deal with anger

"My dear brothers and sisters, take note of this: Everyone should be quick to listen, slow to speak and slow to become angry, because our anger does not produce the righteousness that God desires." (James 1:19-20)

A. Leave the scene.

B. Practice contemplative prayer.

C. Exercise.

D. Write down your thoughts and emotions.

E. Draw. Paint. Do other creative stuff.

F. Take some deep breaths.

G. Rest.

H. Talk to someone you trust.

(Have your guys add additional ideas, if they have any, in the blanks.)

I. _____.

J. _____.

4. When to ask for extra help

(Tell your parents, a teacher, a counselor, or another adult you trust if any of these things have been happening:

▷ You have a lasting feeling of anger over things that have either happened to you in the past or are going on now.

▷ You feel irritable, grumpy, or in a bad mood more often than not.

▷ You feel consistent anger or rage at yourself.

▷ You feel anger lasting for days or making you want to hurt yourself or someone else.

▷ You often get into fights or arguments.)

"Get rid of all bitterness, rage and anger, brawling and slander, along with every form of malice." (Ephesians 4:31)

FEELINGS, PART TWO: HOW TO DEAL WITH YOUR ANGER

"Do not be quickly provoked in your spirit, for anger resides in the lap of fools."
(Ecclesiastes 7:9)

According to the U.S. Department of Justice, men account for _____ percent of all arrests. Men also commit _____ percent of violent crimes.

1. Know what you're f_____.

   A. "Love...is not easily angered." (1 Corinthians 13:4-5)

   B. Instead of anger you may be feeling—

   ▷ g_____ (because you did something wrong or got caught).

   ▷ e_____ (because of something unexpected).

   ▷ p_____ (because someone is putting you down).

   ▷ s_____ (because of something said or done).

   ▷ p_____ (because you did something stupid).

   ▷ some other feeling.

2. All anger isn't the s_____.

   A. Ask yourself: Am I angry because something wrong happened, or am I angry because I'm being s_____?

   B. Two kinds of anger: R_____ anger

   (Motivated by others, by bad things happening)

"[Jesus] looked around at them in anger and, deeply distressed at their stubborn hearts, said to the man, 'Stretch out your hand.' He stretched it out, and his hand was completely restored." (Mark 3:5)

C. Two kinds of anger: S_____ anger

(Selfishly motivated)

"Fools give full vent to their rage, but the wise bring calm in the end." (Proverbs 29:11)

3. Ways to deal with anger

"My dear brothers and sisters, take note of this: Everyone should be quick to listen, slow to speak and slow to become angry, because our anger does not produce the righteousness that God desires." (James 1:19-20)

A. Leave the scene.

B. Practice contemplative prayer.

C. Exercise.

D. Write down your thoughts and emotions.

E. Draw. Paint. Do other creative stuff.

F. Take some deep breaths.

G. Rest.

H. Talk to someone you trust.

I. _____.

J. _____.

4. When to ask for extra help

Tell your parents, a teacher, a counselor, or another adult you trust if any of these things has been happening:

▷ You have a lasting feeling of anger over things that have either happened to you in the past or are going on now.

▷ You feel irritable, grumpy, or in a bad mood more often than not.

▷ You feel consistent anger or rage at yourself.

▷ You feel anger lasting for days or making you want to hurt yourself or someone else.

▷ You're often getting into fights or arguments.

"Get rid of all bitterness, rage and anger, brawling and slander, along with every form of malice." (Ephesians 4:31)

RIGHTEOUS OR SELFISH?

Figuring out whether you're angry because something wrong is happening or because you aren't getting your way can be really hard sometimes.

Read each of the situations below and circle whether you think the anger over the situation is righteous or selfish.

1. All you wanted was to get out of the house to hang out with your friend. Being home is borrrrr-ing. Your mom said no, and now you're mad. Righteous or selfish?

2. Your dad works all the time. You try to spend time with him, but he's always too busy. Every day you ask him how his day was, and his answer is always the same: "Fine." You're mad because your dad is totally unavailable. Righteous or selfish?

3. You're angry because you caught your friend in a lie. He said he couldn't go to your birthday party because he had to go out of town. But you saw him at the movies later on with some other guys from school. Righteous or selfish?

4. Your mom says you can't go to church because of your attitude, and you feel like punching something. Doesn't she understand going to church is a good thing?! Hello?! Now it'll be another week 'til you see your girlfriend Jennifer. Righteous or selfish?

5. You're furious! Your friend just called something "gay" in a joking way. You don't think he meant anything by it, but you just found out your uncle is gay. Calling something "gay" in jest just isn't appropriate anymore. Righteous or selfish?

6. Your little sister was in your room again today. You've told her to stay out, but she doesn't listen. She says she's just borrowing CDs, but you feel as if she's invading your privacy. Righteous or selfish?

SOUL WORK

Next week we're going to talk about girls. Let's begin by studying the biggest ladies' man of the Bible: Solomon.

1. Solomon knew a ton about women. According to 1 Kings 11:3, he had _____ wives and _____ concubines. (Concubines were women who'd have children in the place of wives who couldn't get pregnant.)

2. Read 1 Kings 3:12. God made Solomon w_____.

3. The dude was so smart, stories were told all the time about him. Read one of the most famous: 1 Kings 3:16-28. Whoa!

4. Unfortunately for Solomon, he cared more about pleasing women than God. Read about what happened to him in 1 Kings 11:9-12 and answer this question:

   What did God forbid Solomon to do?

5. Last but not least, in Ecclesiastes 2:1-11, Solomon concluded that as great as women and everything else seem to be, they're all _____.

6. Okay, so Solomon may not be as smart as we once thought. So let's go to the resident expert: Talk to your mom. If your mom isn't around, talk to your grandma or another woman who you respect and ask her these questions: *What are the top-five things I need to know about girls? I mean, what are they looking for in guys? What do I need to know to understand them? How should they be treated?*

   Make sure to write your mom's top-five answers on the back of this sheet and bring them with you next week.

CHAPTER FIVE

THE GIRL CHAPTER: IMPORTANT FACTS ABOUT THE OPPOSITE SEX

THE BIG IDEA

The right way to treat a girl

Main Text

> "Many waters cannot quench love; rivers cannot sweep it away." (Song of Solomon 8:7)

What's the Point?

In this session we'll talk about how girls are wired, what girls wish guys knew about them, and how to treat girls on dates. We'll look at how radical Jesus was with how he treated women and how he gives us a model for our relationships with girls today.

RECAP SOUL WORK

Last week's **Soul Work** was two-fold. The first half focused on Solomon's life and how he was considered wise. Unfortunately for him, he forgot his first love, and God didn't allow him to accomplish his dream—building a temple.

At the end of Solomon's life he concludes that pursuing wealth and women is meaningless. Only wisdom counts.

The second half was interviewing a mom or mom-like person and asking for the top-five things a guy needs to know about girls. Have your guys share the answers from their interviews.

When they're finished, reiterate your focus for this session by saying, **Today we're going to talk about girls. I'll answer as many questions as I can and give you the information you need to know. Let's jump in.**

OPENING ACTIVITY

Option One: Middle School Love Story

The one single trick I've used to keep the attention of middle schoolers is talking about my crushes in middle school. Surely you had at least one, too. Think back to the great gal who made your heart leap out of your chest and your palms sweat the moment you saw her.

Try to remember how it was for you as a middle school student, the feelings you had, the content of the notes you wrote, the nervousness… think back and capture those moments.

Talk about how you felt about girls, what things you knew about them, and the things you were clueless about. Talk about things you were curious about: What do you say on the phone? How do you get off the phone? What happens if she doesn't like me?

Be real. Be tactful. Be honest. And have fun. These are some of my favorite stories to tell because I feel the guys connecting with me.

After you share your story and while your guys are still laughing, transition them to the **Big Picture** by saying something like this, **Girls are crazy. And you think you know so much about them, but let me tell you, you don't know anything. Today we're going to talk about how God wants us to treat girls by seeing how Jesus treated them. Let's pray.**

Option Two: Ladies' Man Scavenger Hunt

Make copies of the **Ladies' Man Scavenger Hunt** sheet. Tell your guys you'll be talking about love this meeting.

To get them going, pass out the Ladies' Man Scavenger Hunt sheet and go over the directions. Once they have a handle on what they're doing, tell them the pages from the magazines are hidden all over the room, then set them free and crown the first guy done "Ladies' Man of the Night" or "Dr. Love."

YOU'LL NEED

Specific pages you've torn out of magazines for the **Ladies' Man Scavenger Hunt** (and make sure they're hidden all over the space in which your group meets), a hat or a bag, copies of a *Breakaway* magazine article titled "Girls 101: Ask the Experts," *The Missing Piece Meets the Big O* by Shel Silverstein

Next transition them into the **Big Picture** by saying something like, **This world of girls can be super confusing. Today we're going to give you some facts about girls to help you feel confident around them and create some of the best relationships you've ever dreamed of. Let's pray together and jump in.**

Option Three: Bag o' Questions

Grab the sheet titled **Bag o' Questions.** Cut out all the questions and throw them in a bag or hat. Feel free to add some great ones of your own. Tell your guys today you're going to talk about girls.

But before we see what God's Word has to say, we want to know what they, the middle school experts, have to say. So go over the game with them and have fun. Have guys take turns picking a question out of the bag. The guy who's up has a choice. He can answer the question or do 10 push-ups.

Once you've finished the questions, are out of time, or giggling has permanently halted the game, transition them to the **Big Picture** by saying something like, **The world of girls can be pretty scary. We don't know so much about girls, being guys and all. Today I'm going to share with you some pretty sweet stuff about girls to help you be able to feel less dorky around them and create some of the best relationships you could ever imagine. Let's pray and get started.**

THE BIG PICTURE

For this part we're diving into three stories from the Gospels about Jesus' interaction with women: the Samaritan woman, the sick woman, and the woman who lived a sinful life. Through these passages you'll be showing your guys how Jesus was the ultimate ladies' man. Those interactions give us an incredible model of interacting with girls.

Introduce the **Outline** by discussing the following two questions:

1. What does it mean if someone is a ladies' man?

2. What were you taught about how to treat girls?

Then say something like, **Today we're going to see how Jesus, the ultimate example of a man, treated women, and what we can learn from his example.**

Once you're done with the **Outline**, transition them with this promise: If you guys can grab hold of what we're learning, not only will you have some of the best relationships with girls ever, but also you'll change the world.

BREAKDOWN
Option One: What Girls Wish Guys Knew

Say, **All right, now that we've looked at Jesus and how he treated women, let's talk about the real deal. What do girls want us guys to know about them?**

Breakaway is a magazine for guys published by Focus on the Family. It's a decent read and has some really great stuff. You can access the article titled "Girls 101: Ask the Experts" online by surfing to www.breakawaymag.com/Girls/A000000076.cfm. If you're able to print it and pass it out to your guys, it'll help them get perspective from some real live girls.

Read through the article together and talk about it. Here are some questions you can use if your guys are stone silent:

▷ **What stood out to you in the article?**

▷ **What surprised you about what the girls say?**

▷ **What do you think you can do differently now that you know this stuff?**

▷ **Tiffany's last piece of advice is, "Don't settle for second best." What do you think she means?**

Lead into the **Closing Activity** by saying something like, **I really like Tiffany's encouragement not to settle for second best. Let's talk about some practical ways we can do that.**

Option Two: Agree or Disagree

This experience should give your guys something to process as well as burn off some energy. You'll be reading a bunch of statements, and the guys will have to decide whether they agree or disagree. Designate one wall in your room as the agree wall and another as the disagree wall and have students go to one wall or the other for each statement.

Introduce this by saying something like, **All right, guys, now that we've talked about how we need to treat girls, I've got some real-world advice here from girls. I want to know whether you agree or disagree with these statements based on what you know about girls.**

Go over the instructions and then go through the list. Feel free to stop between statements to talk about the ones you feel are important for the guys to understand.

▷ **Girls want guys who can fix all their problems.**

▷ **Girls only want guys who have sweet skills.**

▷ **Girls care more about having good friendships than they do about having buff boyfriends.**

▷ **A guy with an awesome car will get a better-looking girlfriend.**

▷ **A guy who is a good flirter doesn't need cheesy pickup lines.**

▷ **A guy who listens is more important than a guy with all the answers.**

▷ **Girls care more about how a guy looks than about who he is as a person.**

▷ **Girls are really impressed if you can burp the alphabet.**

▷ **When out on a date, girls don't mind if you talk about your past girlfriends.**

▷ **The most important skill a guy needs when asking out a girl is confidence.**

After you've burned through the list or your game has turned into a mosh pit, talk about some of your own positive and negative experiences and how you've learned from them.

Move to the **Closing Activity** by saying something like, **Understanding the world of girls is tough. But some things are more important than trying to figure girls out. Let's talk about one of them.**

Option Three: The Dreaded "Best Friend"

Now that we've seen how a real man treats a woman, it's time to see if your guys are up for the challenge. The ol' dreaded best friend challenge.

We've all been there (and if you have a great story for your guys, use it as part of this option). When the girl you have a crush on only likes you as a friend. She has no idea how you feel about her. You've never told her. And now she's fighting with her boyfriend and wants your help.

Tell the guys, **Here's an e-mail "Jessica" has written you:**

> **Hey, bud! How wuz class? I had algebra...BORING. What are you doin' after school? Mike is so lame. He just doesn't get it. I think we're going to break up. But I don't know. I mean, I like him and all, but he doesn't listen much. He's always trying to fix my problems—as if he could! I wonder if I've made the right choice. He's always talking about his past girlfriends. And I get it. He's a great-looking guy. But something just seems to be missing on the inside, you know, the part that really matters. Anyway...you got any thoughts for me? What should I do?**

After you read Jessica's e-mail, ask your guys these questions:

▷ **What does Jessica like about Mike?** *(Possible answer: his looks)*

▷ **What bothers her about him?** *(He's a bad listener. Always tries to fix problems instead of just listening. He talks about his ex-girlfriends.)*

▷ **From what you can tell, what's more important to Jessica: Mike's looks or Mike's personality?** *(Uh, clearly his personality...or not.)*

▷ **What does Jessica's note tell you about what she looks for in a guy?**

▷ **What's your advice to her? Should she dump him or give him another chance?**

▷ **Is this the time you tell her you like her? If so, how do you think she'll feel about you?**

After you rebuke a couple of your boys for deciding it's finally their chance to get a date with Jessica, wrap up this part and move on to the **Closing Activity** by saying something like, **Now that I've given you guys a sneak peak into the mind of a girl, I want to challenge you with one more thing before we end.**

CLOSING ACTIVITY

Option One: Make Your List

End the teaching time in this session about girls by having each guy make a list of what he wants in a girlfriend. Or take it to an even deeper level and have each guy make a list of what he wants in a wife. You can use the handout called **The List** or just give your guys some paper and pens.

Have the guys think about what they're looking for and have them write those qualities down. Does a guy want a girl who's a Christian? Has a good relationship with her parents? Can think for herself?

Then do the next two things:

1. *Encourage your guys not to settle for less.* They're children of the King. And they deserve the best. Challenge them to use their lists as guides for future relationships. If a girl fits the list, she's in. If she doesn't, she's out.

2. *Ask them to pray over the lists.* Remind them that their heavenly Father is the King. The King can give them anything. In John 15:7 Jesus promises us we'll receive whatever we ask for. Encourage them to pray for their future wives or girlfriends using the lists.

Then put the lists in a big pile and end the teaching part of the session by laying hands on the lists and praying for each one of your guys by name. Ask God to help the boys take up the challenge to pray for their future relationships and pass out this week's **Soul Work** sheet.

Option Two: Prayer Partners

End your teaching time by having guys pair up and spend some time in prayer. Encourage the guys to pray for two things:

1. Pray they'll honor God with their bodies by staying pure.

2. Pray for their future wives to stay pure as well and connected to Jesus.

It's one thing to pray for yourself and to pray for your future wife. It's a whole different deal having one of your buddies pray for you and your future wife.

Yes, it may seem hokey. And I'm okay with that. If it gives your guys the idea that somewhere their future wives are out there and that they can start praying for these women now, this can provide some huge perspective for the guys.

Close your time together with a prayer over all of them and then pass out this week's **Soul Work** sheet.

Option Three: *The Missing Piece Meets the Big O*

End your teaching time by reading this book. This great story encourages the reader to enjoy relationships for their own value instead of looking for a relationship to make yourself happy.

Once you're done reading, debrief the book by asking these questions (if you're short on time or your guys are super squirrelly, make the connection for them):

> ▷ **What was the missing piece looking for?**

> ▷ **What makes the Big O so different?**

> ▷ **What's the point of the story?**

> ▷ **How does this relate to the issue of dating?**

Close by saying something like, **Unless you know who and whose you are, you'll never find happiness in a relationship with any girl.**

Hand out the **Soul Work** sheet as well and then end your time in prayer.

OUTLINE (LEADER GUIDE)

THE GIRL CHAPTER: IMPORTANT FACTS ABOUT THE OPPOSITE SEX

"Many waters cannot quench love; rivers cannot sweep it away." Song of Solomon 8:7

(God is the Creator of love. And love is the greatest feeling in the world, which is why we're talking about it.)

Jesus, the Ultimate Ladies' Man

1. Jesus and the <u>Samaritan</u> woman: Read John 4:1-27.

    (The disciples were surprised. Back then Jews didn't hang out with Samaritans. In fact, they're enemies. And no Jewish dude would be caught dead just hanging out with a woman, especially a Samaritan woman. Which leads us to...)

    Jesus demonstrates that the <u>inner life</u> of a woman counts more than her race, her <u>outward</u> condition.

    (You can talk about lots here. Talk about focusing on a girl's "person." A woman's real beauty comes from the kind of person she is, not just her race or what she looks like. Share in your own life how this is true for you.

    For example, a woman may be totally attractive, but if she acts like a jerk, then she loses her appeal. Also, you've probably met lots of women who may not be supermodels, but they're some of the most amazing women you've had the pleasure of knowing—and that alone makes them attractive!)

2. Jesus and the <u>sick</u> woman: Read Mark 5:25-34.

    (Jesus is crushed by the crowd, but he knows something's up. The woman comes up trembling, and Jesus has compassion on her and blesses her. Jesus calls her something other than "Hey, lady!" He says, "Daughter," even though this woman is more than likely older than him. Thus...)

Jesus treated women with <u>honor</u> and <u>respect</u>.

(This is how we're to treat women and girls. We should make them feel special and extraordinary. This can mean anything from opening doors for them to being sensitive about what you talk about in their presence.)

3. Jesus and the woman who lived a *sinful* life: Read Luke 7:36-50.

Jesus treats her as a <u>person</u> instead of a <u>piece of meat</u>.

(When most guys think about girls, their thoughts center more on their bodies and looks than on who they are as people. Jesus treated women as equals, not as objects.)

Transition to the **Breakdown** with something like, **Now that we have a model to follow, let's take it one more step.**

BAG O' QUESTIONS

Cut out these questions and put them in a hat or bag of some sort. Have guys take turns picking a question out of the bag. The guy who's up has a choice: He can answer the question he draws or do 10 push-ups.

Who's the prettiest girl at your school and why?

Who would you rather date and why—a cruel, pretty girl or a cool girl who just looks okay?

How old should you be to go on a date and why?

Give me an idea of a really great date.

If money were no expense, what would you do for a date?

When you see a pretty girl, what's the first thing you notice and why?

What's the most important thing you look for in a girl and why?

Finish this sentence: The one question I have about girls is...

Finish this sentence: Guys and girls are mostly different because...

What's the stupidest thing you've ever said to a girl?

Finish this sentence: The worst thing about girls is...

Who's your best friend (who's a girl), and what makes her so cool?

Would you rather go on a date with a big group of people or just one? Why?

What's the worst kind of food to eat on a date and why?

What should you never do on a date? Name three things.

How long should you have to date until you hold hands?

How long should you have to date until you hug?

How long should you have to date until you kiss?

LADIES' MAN SCAVENGER HUNT

There are magazine pages scattered and hidden all over the space where you're meeting. Go find them, taking this sheet with you. Look for magazine pages with the following 10 things. Be the first one done and claim your prize as Doctor Love, the real ladies' man.

1. A beautiful girl.

2. The word *love*.

3. A couple holding hands.

4. Cologne or perfume.

5. A photo of some grub.

6. A rock. You need a photo of some jewelry you need to give this girl.

7. A word that rhymes with "romance."

8. Some lips or people kissing.

9. How about the dream car you hope to pick up your dream date with?

10. Don't forget...you'll need some flowers. Find a photo of one and slap it down on the pile to win.

THE GIRL CHAPTER: IMPORTANT FACTS ABOUT THE OPPOSITE SEX

"Many waters cannot quench love; rivers cannot sweep it away." (Song of Solomon 8:7)

Jesus, the Ultimate Ladies' Man

1. Jesus and the S_____ woman: Read John 4:1-27.

   Jesus demonstrated that the i_____ counts more than her race, her o_____.

2. Jesus and the s_____ woman: Read Mark 5:25-34.

   Jesus treated women with h_____ and r_____.

3. Jesus and the woman who lived a s_____ life: Read Luke 7:36-50.

   Jesus treats her as a p_____ instead of a p_____.

From *Living as a Young Man of God* by Ken Rawson. Permission to reproduce this page granted only for use in buyer's youth group. Copyright ©2008 by Youth Specialties.

THE LIST

1. _____

2. _____

3. _____

4. _____

5. _____

6. _____

7. _____

8. _____

9. _____

10. _____

SOUL WORK

Talking about girls leads us to what we'll talk about next week: Temptation and lust.

1. What have you heard in church or read in the Bible about temptation and lust?

2. Read 1 Corinthians 10:13 and rewrite the verse in your own words.

3. Now read Colossians 3:5-6 and 1 Corinthians 6:18-20 and rewrite the passages in your own words.

4. Based on what the Bible says about temptation and lust, how do you think they're connected? Are they both sins in God's eyes?

CHAPTER SIX

DEALING WITH TEMPTATION AND LUST

> **Very Important Leader Note:**
>
> This session will provide an opportunity to give your guys real-world help on issues many middle school students face.
>
> While this can be a GREAT opportunity, it also may pose problems. In particular, some parents may be hesitant to have you teach on this subject because they feel unprepared to discuss with their sons or simply don't believe their boys are ready for it.
>
> So in addition to running this session's topic past your supervisor, *please*, please, please contact parents at least a week before your small group meeting and initiate the conversation. Go over with them what you're planning to share with their sons. *Encourage parents by telling them you'll provide a list of questions for their boys to further the discussion at home (that's this week's* **Soul Work***)*. Ask how you can help them. Your phone calls to parents will communicate your care, earn their trust, and help your guys create bridges with their parents about these important issues. IMPORTANT: If any parent doesn't want the session done at all, consult with your supervisor on what steps to take next.

THE BIG IDEA

Help your guys deal with temptation and lust.

Main Text

> "Create in me a pure heart, O God, and renew a steadfast spirit within me." (Psalm 51:10)

What's the Point?

This session will focus on the issues of temptation, lust, and purity. More than anything we want to challenge guys to live pure lives because of their identities, because of who and whose they are. We'll see how Jesus radically taught about purity and lived a pure life.

YOU'LL NEED

A quarter; some scratch paper; some vanilla ice cream, strawberry syrup, paper bowls, and some plastic spoons

RECAP SOUL WORK

Last week your guys had a few tasks to complete for their **Soul Work**. Ask them also to share how they rewrote 1 Corinthians 6:18-20 in their own words.

When you're ready, transition by saying, **Today we're going to take a deeper look into this issue and hopefully answer some of your biggest questions about it.**

OPENING ACTIVITY

Option One: Quarter Challenge

Having a serious conversation about lust with middle school guys is a challenge in and of itself. Introduce the subject with a challenge of your own.

Now that your guys are getting pretty manly, have three of them step up for the "quarter challenge."[6] Have one guy at a time stand with his back against the wall. Make sure his heels are against the wall as well.

Next place a quarter on the floor between his feet. Tell him if he can get the quarter, he can have it. The only catch is he can't bend his legs, and he can't touch the wall with his hands. (The task is pretty much impossible unless the student brings a chair over in front of him and uses it for balance. Then he should be able to do it.)

When the challenge is over, transition to the **Big Picture** by saying something like, **Your lives are full of challenges as you become men. One of the more difficult challenges you'll experience over and over again in your lives is not letting temptations turn into lust. Today we'll talk about ways to face that challenge head-on.**

Open up your group in prayer and jump in.

[6]Adapted from "Way of Escape" from Michael Kast's *100 Middle School Games & Activities*. Louisville, KY: Southeast Christian Church.

Option Two: Your Story and Questions

This issue of dealing with temptation and lust can be difficult for students who are embarrassed, or whose parents don't talk about these subjects, or who've been filled with so much misinformation from the media and hearsay from friends that they're way past confused. Your time together is so valuable, so you may want to give your guys some time to ask some real questions and get real answers.

To help break the ice, you can do the previous option, or you might just share honestly from your life. You can even inject some appropriate humor and help ease the tension.

Here's what I say sometimes: **All right, guys, tonight we're talking about temptation and lust. I'm guessing most of you think you have it all pretty much figured out and don't need any help. That's how I felt when I was in middle school, but I was always glad when someone would ask a question.**

Go on with a personal story that illustrates the difficulties you had—to whatever degree—feeling comfortable talking about dealing with temptation and lust.

Finish with, **So today I want to give you the opportunity to ask any question you want. Nothing is off-limits. There's no stupid question. You don't have to put your name on your question. And if I can't answer it today, I'll try to next week.**

Then pass out slips of scratch paper and pencils and give the guys time to write down a question or two. If your guys are like mine, this can be an exercise in futility as they'll all look around to see if someone else is writing...then one will giggle...then another...yeah, you know how it is.

If they don't write anything, don't worry. This part is just to get them thinking. If they're hesitant, say something like, **Hey, I see you guys don't have any huge questions you want to share right now, so we'll move on. But keep the paper, and if you think of something, write it down.**

At the end of this session you'll have an opportunity to answer questions, too. Open up your group in prayer and move on to the **Big Picture.**

THE BIG PICTURE

As we've seen from Scripture, God wants us to have pure minds and bodies. But in our Internet-driven culture with its preoccupation with sex, it's hard to get this message across and have it mean anything to youth. Temptation is all around us; lust often follows right behind.

In short, our culture doesn't care too much about temptation because lust is viewed as okay—in fact, lust is a good thing to many people. A fair number of Christians would probably agree—which can make teaching about dealing with temptation and fighting against lust a losing battle.

So the first step is to get your guys talking about the issues they're facing—get the discussion going through the **Outline** and help your guys really consider what you're suggesting.

Please don't get bogged down with wanting to cover every sort of purity illustration you've ever heard, trying to get the guys to stop watching R-rated movies, or bribing them to read every say-no-to-sex book available.

Trust God to work through this overview, your guarded transparency, and the gentle prodding of the Holy Spirit.

BREAKDOWN
Lust Sundae

Tell your guys you're going to reward them for doing such a great job listening, taking notes, and not completely destroying the **Outline** by practicing their origami skills on it. The start scooping the ice cream and make your guys some small strawberry sundaes. And while you're dishing out sundaes, share this fun illustration[7]:

> **Have you ever thought about what you're putting in your mouth when you eat a delicious ice cream sundae? Never mind the calories or the fat grams—we're talking about some serious ingredients.**
>
> **For example, today's commercial ice cream usually substitutes dimethyl glycol instead of eggs—a chemical also used in antifreeze and paint remover. Most of the time, piperonal is substituted for vanilla, but it's also used in larger quantities to kill lice.**

[7] Rice, Wayne. Hot Illustrations for Youth Talks on CD-ROM Version 1.0. Grand Rapids, MI: Zondervan, 2001.

And then when you top off the sundae with strawberry flavor, remember you're probably ingesting benzyl acetate, a chemical used as a solvent for nitrate, one of the main ingredients in fertilizers and cheap explosives.

This information shouldn't stop us from eating ice cream or make us want to start boycotting Dairy Queen. Ice cream is fine and wonderful as long as we enjoy it the way it's made. But if we just decide we're hungry for ice cream and start scarfing down antifreeze and lice medi-cine, we'd probably die (although it might be with a nice clean scalp and a circulation sys-tem not affected by cold weather).

Why would we die? Because we'd be attempt-ing to quench a normal desire for ice cream in a way never intended by ice cream makers.

Lust can be an awful lot like ice cream.

You see, lust is any desire that leads us to satis-fy a normal hunger in a way never intended by our Maker. Lust is what happens when good, God-given appetites consume us, control us, and become our points of focus—so we try to satisfy our God-given appetite in a way God didn't design. That's what happens when we let lust into our minds and hearts.

Transition to the **Closing Activity** by saying something like, **As we close tonight, I have one more thing I want to share with you.**

CLOSING ACTIVITY
Option One: Accountability Group

Challenge your guys to take this issue of purity seriously by encouraging them to get involved in an accountability group. This option isn't your final word on accountability, as it's covered more in the next chapter.

Say something like, **Living a pure life isn't easy. That's why I want to challenge you to get involved in some kind of accountability group. An accountability group is two or more guys who meet together regularly for encouragement in regard to keeping a pure mind and body.**

If you meet in an accountability group, this would be a great time to share from your life about how being in an accountability group has helped you. Next pass out the **Tips for Accountability Groups** sheet.

As you finish, draw the guys' attention to the verse at the bottom of the sheet. Remind them of God's gift of grace and forgiveness. And encourage them to pray for God's grace and forgiveness as they commit to living pure lives.

Hand out and go over this week's **Soul Work** sheet (it involves parents, so encourage your guys to talk with their parents) and close by praying David's words in Psalm 51:10 out loud together. His words are really our words.

Option Two: Questions

If you chose to do this option from the **Opening Activity**, this would be a great time to answer some of those questions. Whether you used that option earlier or not, you may feel the need to spend the rest of your time answering your guys' questions.

If so, be honest; if you're not sure of an answer, tell them you'll try to answer the question next week.

When you run out of questions or time, draw their attention back to their **Outline**. At the very bottom is a verse King David wrote while he was repenting of his affair with Bathsheba. His words are really our words.

Remind them of God's gifts of grace and forgiveness. Affirm your guys' pursuit of purity and make David's prayer from Psalm 51:10 your closing prayer. Read it together out loud.

Finally, hand out and go over this week's **Soul Work** sheet. It involves parents so encourage your guys to talk with their parents.

SHAME-BASED FEELINGS

Usually the idea of sharing our hearts and failures with students is met with shame. We worry that our stories will give our guys one more reason to justify their sins. "Well, Bob messed around as a teenager. And he's all right. I guess that's okay for me, too."

Instead what happens is, your guys see you as a real person, and as they see the regret in your eyes, they'll have one more reason why they don't ever want to feel the way you do about whatever subject you share about.

Transparency breeds intimacy and life change. Remember, you don't need to tell the guys all of your mistakes. But take a chance to let them know you're a mere mortal who understands the power, lure, and temptation of sex.

Option Three: Commit to Purity

Challenge your guys to be pure. Purity is about honoring God, respecting our bodies, and living holy lives.

If you're up for it, share part of your story. Share about some of the mistakes you've made along the way (without being specific or graphic). Next draw the guys' attention back to the **Outline**. At the very bottom is a verse King David wrote while he was repenting of his affair with Bathsheba. His words are really our words.

Remind them of God's gifts of grace and forgiveness. Affirm your guys' pursuit of purity and make David's prayer from Psalm 51:10 your closing prayer. Read it together out loud.

Finally, hand out and go over this week's **Soul Work** sheet. It involves parents so encourage your guys to talk with their parents.

OUTLINE (LEADER GUIDE)

DEALING WITH TEMPTATION AND LUST
What's the difference between them?

1. Jesus was tempted in the <u>desert</u>.

   Read Matthew 4:1-11, the account of Satan's temptation of Jesus in the desert outside of Jerusalem—an ordeal that lasted 40 days!

2. Jesus experienced the same <u>struggles</u> with temptation that we face.

   Read Hebrews 4:15 for a shocking revelation!

   (As you can see, Jesus was hit with every temptation we've been hit with—and a few others that we'll never probably face, such as Satan taking us to a high place and telling us all the kingdoms of the world can be ours if we just bow down to him. If it was okay for Jesus to be tempted, it's definitely not a sin when we find ourselves tempted to sin. True, it's zero fun and makes for struggles at times, but don't ever forget—when you're being tempted, you're not sinning! Don't let anyone tell you differently.)

3. Lust is when you allow your temptations to turn into unhealthy fixations on whatever it is you're attracted to (girls, money, popularity—you name it). Lust is definitely <u>sin</u>.

   Keys to dealing with lust

   1. A pure <u>mind</u>

   A. Read Matthew 5:28. Jesus says, "Anyone who looks at a woman <u>lustfully</u> has already committed adultery with her in his heart."

   In this case, lust is when you have an intense, unhealthy sexual desire—and as followers of Jesus, we mustn't allow lust in our lives.

   (Jesus is saying when you look at a female who isn't your wife with intense sexual desire, in your heart you're committing the same sin as adultery—when married couples are unfaithful to each other. Whoa! Hold on a second, Jesus! We aren't talking about noticing whether a girl is attractive or pretty or even liking her. Instead looking lustfully at a female means your desire for a girl is really your desire to satisfy yourself.)

   Here are some examples of lust:

   ▷ Looking down a girl's shirt

   ▷ Staring at a girl's body

▷ Thinking of a girl in sexual ways

▷ Imagining having sex or doing sexual things

▷ Thinking of a girl as a sexual object

▷ Watching nude scenes in movies

(Our brains are so powerful that they store all those thoughts and images, and you'll be amazed at how easily they can be retrieved. So the first way to deal with lust is by having a pure mind—and not putting yourselves in positions or situations when lust can happen. When you sense lust starting, do your best to get out of the situation you find yourself in.)

2. A pure <u>body</u>

(What's the most expensive thing you own? How do you treat it? Why are you so careful with it? Because it's valuable, right? Your body is incredibly valuable, and it's a big part of the second way to deal with lust: Keeping your body pure. Look at this next verse from 1 Corinthians.)

"Flee from sexual immorality. All other sins people commit are outside their bodies, but those who sin sexually sin against their own bodies. Do you not know that your bodies are temples of the Holy Spirit, who is in you, whom you have received from God? You are not your own; you were bought at a price. Therefore honor God with your bodies." (6:18-20)

(Your bodies are special houses for the Holy Spirit. They aren't even yours. God gives them to you to use...on loan. How many of you guys would take a library book and tear out the pages or throw it in the mud? Yeah, of course not. And how much more valuable are you than a library book?

When you keep your body pure, you're keeping lust at bay—as well as a whole bunch of bad situations that can happen because lust got a foothold in your mind and heart. A real man keeps his body pure.)

This last verse is for the **Closing Activity**. Skip it and move on to the **Breakdown**.

"Create in me a pure heart, O God, and renew a steadfast spirit within me." (Psalm 51:10)

DEALING WITH TEMPTATION AND LUST
What's the difference between them?

1. Jesus was tempted in the d_____.

    Read Matthew 4:1-11, the account of Satan's temptation of Jesus in the desert outside of Jerusalem—an ordeal that lasted 40 days!

2. Jesus experienced the same s_____ with temptation that we face.

    Read Hebrews 4:15 for a shocking revelation!

3. Lust is when you allow your temptations to turn into unhealthy fixations on whatever it is you're attracted to (girls, money, popularity—you name it). Lust is definitely s_____.

    Keys to dealing with lust

    1. A pure _____

    A. Read Matthew 5:28. Jesus says, "Anyone who looks at a woman _____ has already committed adultery with her in his heart."

    In this case, lust is when you have an intense, unhealthy sexual desire—and as followers of Jesus, we mustn't allow lust in our lives.

    Here are some examples of lust:

    ▷   Looking down a girl's shirt

    ▷   Staring at a girl's body

    ▷   Thinking of a girl in sexual ways

    ▷   Imagining having sex or doing sexual things

    ▷   Thinking of a girl as a sexual object

    ▷   Watching nude scenes in movies

2. A pure <u>body</u>

"Flee from sexual immorality. All other sins people commit are outside their bodies, but those who sin sexually sin against their own bodies. Do you not know that your bodies are temples of the Holy Spirit, who is in you, whom you have received from God? You are not your own; you were bought at a price. Therefore honor God with your bodies." (1 Corinthians 6:18-20)

This last verse is for the **Closing Activity**. Skip it and move on to the **Breakdown**.

"Create in me a pure heart, O God, and renew a steadfast spirit within me." (Psalm 51:10)

TIPS FOR ACCOUNTABILITY GROUPS

Connect each day in person, on the phone, by e-mail, or by texting.

Ask your partners how they're doing today (at keeping their minds and bodies pure).

Be real.

Be honest.

Encourage each other.

"Create in me a pure heart, O God, and renew a steadfast spirit within me." (Psalm 51:10)

TIPS FOR ACCOUNTABILITY GROUPS

Connect each day in person, on the phone, by e-mail, or by texting.

Ask your partners how they're doing today (at keeping their minds and bodies pure).

Be real.

Be honest.

Encourage each other.

"Create in me a pure heart, O God, and renew a steadfast spirit within me." (Psalm 51:10)

SOUL WORK

I'm sure the last thing you want to do is talk to your parents about temptation and lust. Many parents are just as uncomfortable talking about these issues with their kids. Believe it or not, some parents don't say anything to their children about these subjects. Use the following questions to open up about this subject with your parents.

One more thing before you jump in: Be honest and real. Your parents really want to help you, but if they think you're not dealing with this stuff, they'll treat you as if you aren't.

Remember, your parents were middle schoolers once, too. And you might be surprised at what they were dealing with when they were your age.

1. Have everyone (you and your parents) finish this sentence: "Talking about temptation and lust makes me feel _____ because _____."

2. Ask your parents, "When you were in middle school, what were some of the questions you were dealing with about lust?"

3. Ask your dad or an older Christian man you trust, "What are some ways you try to keep your mind pure?"

At some point, you're going to need and want your parents' input. You'll want to feel as if you can ask them anything. Maybe you feel that way now. If so, that's great!

But you may not feel that way in the years to come. And your parents are going to want to be able to ask you open and honest questions without you feeling as if they're prying into your personal life. Which brings us to the next question:

4. Ask your parents, "How can we as a family develop a relationship where we both feel free to talk and ask questions about this issue in the future?"

CHAPTER SEVEN

BECOMING A BAND OF BROTHERS

THE BIG IDEA

You are meant to be part of a band of brothers.

Main Text

> "Because we loved you so much, we were delighted to share with you not only the gospel of God but our lives as well." (1 Thessalonians 2:8)

What's the Point?

We can't walk this life alone. Each of us needs a group of guys who will love us, be there for us, challenge us, and keep us accountable. We'll take a look at the motley crew Jesus called his disciples and relate them to the idea of a band of brothers—so well illustrated in the military and in church history.

Next week is your last week with your guys, and one of the options you can choose will be having a rite-of-passage ceremony. An important part of this ceremony is for your guys to hear from their dads or other significant men in their lives.

At the end of this chapter, you'll find a sample letter to send to your guys' dads (or other significant men—know your guys), which will serve as an invitation to the last part of next week's session as a surprise. The letter will also ask the adults to prepare some kind of affirmation for their sons as they move from being boys to young men.

Please don't send this home with your students. Mail the letter to their dads to keep the surprise a secret.

One more thing: After sending out the letters, please follow up with the dads by phone. The worst thing besides having some of the dads not show up next week for the ceremony is being the boy whose dad didn't show up because the youth leader sent the invitation to the wrong house.

If a dad can't get out of work or has some other commitment, that's totally understandable. Still encourage him to do the affirmation and to choose a special time before your next small group meeting to share it with his son.

If a dad doesn't show up because you mailed the letter to the wrong address or the letter was lost or dad never opened it or whatever, it'll be a very memorable night for your student. However, not in a good way.

YOU'LL NEED

A veteran to talk about his experience in the armed services and, if he's willing, to share about what it means to have a band of brothers; *Saving Private Ryan* DVD; poster board, paper, markers, and any other poster-type creative stuff; supplies to create some kind of unifying, lasting memento for your band of brothers (see the sidebar "Swag for Your Band" for more details on what to get)

RECAP SOUL WORK

Last week your guys more than likely had very uncomfortable talks with their parents about lust. Hopefully, the conversations may've started off awkwardly but ended up being really helpful and paving the way for future conversations.

Greet your guys and ask them how they did on their **Soul Work**. Here are some questions you can use to get the conversation going:

▷ **How did the talk go with your parents?**

▷ **Did you find it helpful?**

▷ **Do you feel as if next time you have a question you can talk to them?**

▷ **What did you decide to do to help all of you talk about these issues in the future?**

Congratulate them on doing a good job and promise them this week's **Soul Work** isn't nearly as difficult.

OPENING ACTIVITY

Option One: Human Knot

Get your guys thinking about working together and becoming one by having them unravel a human knot. Have your guys form a circle. Next have them stick their right arms in the middle and grab the hand of someone across from them but not next to them.

Then have them all put their left hands in the middle and grab someone else's hand in the circle. The only catch is these hands can't belong to those next to them or the same people holding their right hands.

Now they simply have to unravel the knot without breaking their grips. One more catch...no talking. Have them start over if they break their grips. If you have a student who keeps talking, put a blindfold on him.

Once they get unraveled, ask them some of these questions:

▷ **What was the hardest part of unraveling the human knot?**

▷ **Grade yourselves A, B, C, D, or F on how hard you tried.**

▷ **How did you feel being connected and stuck and tangled?**

▷ **How difficult was it to keep your grip?**

▷ **Grade yourselves A, B, C, D, or F on how well you worked together as a group.**

▷ **What would have made this easier?**

Tell your guys **Good job!** and transition them to the **Big Picture** by saying something like, **Eventually, you guys worked together as a team. You got connected with each other and helped each other unravel the knot. As Christians we should connect with each other and share life together.**

Go on, **As we'll see today, Jesus lived that way, the church was created that way, and really, our model for life today is living as a band of brothers the way they did.**

Option Two: Veteran Guest Speaker

Ask your volunteer veteran about his experience in the armed services. Have him share with your guys about what it means to have a band of brothers. If you know a veteran who's seen combat, your illustration may be even more dramatic. If you get a World War II veteran, you earn 2,500 points.

Introduce your speaker by saying, **Having a band of brothers is about having a group of guys you can count on for anything and everything. Guys who'll stick up for you. Guys who'd give their lives for you. A lot of men experience this kind of brotherhood in the armed services. Today I want you to hear from one of them.**

After your guest speaker is done, thank him and applaud and transition to the **Big Picture** with something like, **We should be a band of brothers. As we'll see today, Jesus lived that way, the church was created that way, and really, our model for life today is living as a band of brothers the way they did.**

Option Three: *Saving Private Ryan*[8]

Help your guys get a feeling for the love and commitment behind a group of men who are a band of brothers by showing them this clip from *Saving Private Ryan*.

Set up the clip by saying, **Private Ryan is one of four brothers overseas during World War II. All his brothers died in battle, and the government orders a group of soldiers back behind enemy lines to save Private Ryan so the family doesn't lose all their sons.** (Start the clip at 2:36:00, "They're tank busters, sir, P-51s"; stop at 2:42:00, an American flag waves in the wind.)

Ask some of these questions when the clip is over:

▷ **Captain John Miller and many others died to save Private Ryan. Do you think his life was worth those other men dying? Why or why not?**

▷ **Would you ever die in someone else's place?**

▷ **How do Captain Miller's last words to Private Ryan make you feel?**

▷ **How are Captain Miller's words different from Jesus' words about the sacrifice he made for us?**

▷ **Do you have any friends who would willingly trade their lives for yours given a similar situation? Would you give your life for the life of one of your friends?**

[8] Fields, Doug, and Eddie James. *Videos That Teach 4*. Grand Rapids, MI: Zondervan, 2006.

GUEST-SPEAKER TIP

Whoever you ask to speak wants to do a great job. The best thing you can do is be clear about what you want from him.

In this case, have him talk about how he experienced a feeling similar to having a band of brothers in the military.

If you haven't heard your speaker's story, it may be easier to control the conversation by interviewing him.

Interviewing also relieves some of the pressure for him. After all, he'd just be answering questions.

> What does it take to build a band of brothers type of relationship, such as those men had for Private Ryan?

After you're done, move to the **Big Picture** with something like, **We need friendships like that—bands of brothers. As we'll see today, Jesus lived that way, the church was created that way, and really, our model for life today is living as a band of brothers the way they did.**

THE BIG PICTURE

The **Big Picture** focuses on the love and commitment Jesus had with his disciples and how that love radically birthed the church as we know it.

Who were the disciples? Twelve guys with one purpose: following Jesus. They were committed to him, and he was committed to them. Even to death.

The love, commitment, and relationship they shared together fueled the church as we know it today. Unfortunately, the church hasn't always been so good at living out that kind of love. However, we, your guys included, were created to be part of the Christian band of brothers and restore the church to its original state.

Go through your **Outlines** and then move to the **Breakdown**.

BREAKDOWN

Option One: Hard Questions

Help your guys dig a little deeper into this idea of what being a band of brothers means by asking them some of these questions:

> **Do you have a few really good friends who are kind of your band of brothers?**

> **What would you want your band of brothers to be like?**

> **What makes it hard to trust other guys?**

> **Why is being a loyal friend so important?**

> **What are some things a band of brothers could help you with?**

> **What would make you the kind of friend someone would want to have in his band of brothers?**

After the questions are done, move to the **Closing Activity** by saying something like, **Having a band of brothers is vital to growing in your faith and becoming real men.**

Option Two: Match the Bands

Bands of brothers aren't anything new, and certainly different kinds of brotherhoods exist. Hand your guys copies of **Match the Bands** and go over the instructions. (Answers: 1. H, 2. F, 3. G, 4. E, 5. I, 6. J, 7. A, 8. D, 9. C, 10. B.)

Transition to the **Closing Activity** by saying, **As you can see, all sorts of groups of guys are bands of brothers. As Christians we should be the strongest band of brothers, as when the church began.**

Option Three: Wesley's Band

The founder of the United Methodist Church, John Wesley, was serious about the relationships found in bands of brothers. His focus was on intense accountability and pursuing holiness. His small groups were called "bands" or "societies." Not surprisingly, Wesley had a method for how these bands should conduct their meetings and operate.

His questions are intense and provide a good starting point for students to consider what the focus of their bands should be. They might even consider asking each other some of the questions. I've tried to modernize his original language to something adolescent students can understand and appreciate.

Say something like, **Since we're talking about bands of brothers, I thought I'd share with you about a guy who was really serious about his own band of brothers.**

Then pass out the copies of **John Wesley's "Band of Brothers"** and read through the first half together. You can decide whether you want to work through the questions as a group or have each student complete them on his own and then share. I've done it both ways.

After you've worked through the questions, move to the **Closing Activity** with something like, **When you have a band of brothers committed to standing by you through the good times and bad times, helping you grow in your faith, you have a group of friends you'll have forever.**

CLOSING ACTIVITY

Option One: A Special Band of Brothers

Bring your time to a close by reading 1 Thessalonians 2:8 out loud together. It's on the very bottom of the **Outline**.

Then share this story. Set it up by saying something like, **We've talked a lot today about what it means to be part of a band of brothers. We just read about how Paul felt about his friends. He shared his life with them. Before we close, I want to share with you one last story of some friends who also knew how to share life together.**

Colin was your typical Kansas middle schooler. He had a bunch of friends, loved to watch wrestling, and couldn't live without his basketball. For a couple months Colin had noticed a bump on his leg. He thought it was just a bug bite or something and pretty much ignored it until he hurt his leg playing basketball, and this bump got really swollen.

Colin waited a few days for the swelling to go down, and after it didn't, he went to the hospital. There the doctors didn't like what they saw. Colin had cancer, and the bump was a tumor the size of an orange.

Colin immediately had to undergo chemotherapy to shrink the tumor so it could be removed. Here this tough, wrestling-watching, basketball-playing, fun-loving, strong middle school kid was stuck in a hospital bed, wondering whether he was going to live or die. And then he lost all his hair.

One day he got a call from one of his friends, Eric, who wanted to know if he could come up to the hospital to see him. Colin was bored and totally excited to see his friend, who he hadn't seen for more than a week. He could hardly wait, except he was a little embarrassed about his bald head.

After a couple of hours someone knocked on the door, and in walked Eric and eight of Colin's best friends, and they'd all shaved their heads. Colin not only got to see his friends, but also he knew that no matter what, these guys were going to stand by his side.

Where to take it from here: **Colin's friends could've easily just gone to the hospital and hung out with Colin. But when they shaved their heads, they were saying to Colin, "We're with you. We're in this with you. We're here for you. You're not alone."**

Then say, **What a powerful demonstration of love and loyalty. This is how the church is supposed to be. We should be there for each other. Stand up for one another. Hurt together and laugh together. That's what having a band of brothers is about.**

Close your time together by handing them this week's **Soul Work** sheet and having a student close your time in prayer.

Option Two: Make Your Own Band

If your guys haven't had a chance yet to consider starting their own band of brothers, end your time helping them create rules and questions for their group.

You might say, **I want each one of you guys to have a band of brothers. And I'll start it with me. I'll do whatever I can to help you guys grow in your faith. And I'll try to be here for you. Why don't we start our own band of brothers?**

If your guys aren't into the idea, talk about why they're hesitant. Are they tired? Do they think they don't need a band of brothers? Are they embarrassed? Do they even understand? Do they just have to go to the bathroom bad?

If they're game, use the poster board and art stuff to make your list of how your group is going to work and what questions you want to ask each other. You can even use the questions to open up your small group next week.

Once you're finished with your masterpiece, bring your time to a close by reading 1 Thessalonians 2:8 out loud together. It's on the very bottom of the **Outline**. Talk about how Paul didn't simply tell people about Jesus but shared his life with them, living as part of a band of brothers.

Then tell your guys how proud you are of them, hand them this week's **Soul Work** sheet, and have a student close your time in prayer.

Option Three: Band Swag

Make some kind of special necklace, bracelet, ring, pin, or some kind of rallying piece of swag your guys can have to remind them of their band of brothers.

In *Becoming a Young Man of God*, I give an idea of making necklaces for your guys to encourage good attendance. When one of my small group leaders told me this idea for making his guys necklaces, I was like, "Sure, Bob. That's great. Go for it." You know—knowing the guys would think it was hokier and lamer than I did.

I couldn't have been more wrong. All these necklaces consisted of was a long piece of leather (like a shoelace) and a generic pendant. Then each week the guys came, they were given beads to put on their necklaces.

Our guys LOVED this, and the necklaces became a kind of unifier for them. They felt as if they were part of a super secret society only known to them. And they wore the necklaces proudly each Wednesday night. I've listed a number of ways to create this idea for your guys, depending on your cash flow, in the "Swag for Your Band" sidebar.

If you decide to go this route, make it a big deal. Tell your guys how proud you are of them and their dedication to your small group and how pumped you are to be included in their band of brothers.

After you give them their mementos, close by reading 1 Thessalonians 2:8 out loud together. It's on the very bottom of the **Outline**. Talk about how Paul didn't simply tell people about Jesus but shared his life with them, living as part of a band of brothers.

Then hand them this week's **Soul Work** sheet and have the oldest student close your time in prayer.

SWAG FOR YOUR BAND

If you have lots of cash: All sorts of necklaces, bracelets, and rings can be found at your local Christian retail store. Some of these can be really pricey, and some can be more moderate. Someone in your church may be willing to purchase these for your guys if she understands what you're trying to do.

If you have minimal cash: Find a jeweler who understands what you're trying to do and ask if he can make some low-cost metal jewelry for your guys.

If you have even less cash: Run to your local craft store and pick up a $4 roll of leather string and a $3 variety pack of beads.

Have no cash? Make up some kind of sweet secret handshake only known to your band.

SAMPLE LETTER TO DADS

Dear Dad,

Hi. This is [your name] from church. I've had an incredible time having your son in my small group. We've been talking for a number of weeks about becoming a young man of God and living as a young man of God. Next week we'll be done.

But I need your help. Next week we'll spend the last 20 minutes of our small group time with a special surprise ceremony for your sons, and I'd like you to play the most important part.

Would you please write some kind of affirmation for your son and be prepared to read it to him during that time—something encouraging about how he's entering a new stage of life: Manhood.

If you don't know what to say, you can tell him how proud you are of him and talk about some ways he's shown real maturity. Encourage him to continue seeking Jesus as his model for being a man. Let him know you're going to treat him like a man and expect more from him. Last of all make sure you tell him you love him. Help him know he's special, and he's going to grow into a fine young man.

Also, if you know of other key men in your son's life, I'd encourage you to talk to them and have them write some affirmations as well. You can't have enough men take part in this ceremony. They're welcome to attend as well as to share.

Will you please join us for the very last 20 minutes of our small group time next week? Let's make this an incredible and memorable time your son will be able to tell his children about someday.

If you have any questions, please call me ASAP at [your phone number] or drop me an e-mail at [your e-mail]. See you [date of last meeting].

Sincerely,

[signature]

P.S.: Remember, your son has no idea about this. Please keep this a surprise!

OUTLINE (LEADER GUIDE)

BECOMING A BAND OF BROTHERS

1. Jesus' band of brothers

   (When Jesus was here on earth, he had a group of guys as his band of brothers. Some were fishermen; at least one guy was a tax collector. They were his best friends.)

   A. Who were they? <u>Twelve</u> guys. <u>One</u> purpose: <u>following</u> Jesus.

   "When morning came, he called his disciples to him and chose twelve of them, whom he also designated apostles: Simon (whom he named Peter), his brother Andrew, James, John, Philip, Bartholomew, Matthew, Thomas, James son of Alphaeus, Simon who was called the Zealot, Judas son of James, and Judas Iscariot, who became a traitor." (Luke 6:13-18)

   (Jesus had all kinds of followers, but of them all, he chose 12 to share his life with. They traveled together, ate together, slept in the same rooms together, laughed together, worshiped together. They shared everything. Imagine you and 12 of your buddies on a constant road trip. That was Jesus' life. And their commitment to each other was unmistakable.)

   B. They were committed to <u>him</u>.

   "Peter replied, 'Even if all fall away on account of you, I never will.' 'Truly I tell you,' Jesus answered, 'this very night, before the rooster crows, you will disown me three times.' But Peter declared, 'Even if I have to die with you, I will never disown you.' And all the other disciples said the same." (Matthew 26:33-35)

   (Peter gets a bad rap for denying Jesus. But he had no idea how the night of Jesus' death would play out. You can tell from his words and the words of the other disciples, these guys loved Jesus and were willing to do anything for him. Anything.)

   C. He was committed to <u>them</u>.

   "You see, at just the right time, when we were still powerless, Christ died for the ungodly. Very rarely will anyone die for a righteous person, though for a good person someone might possibly dare to die. But God demonstrates his own love for us in this: While we were still sinners, Christ died for us." (Romans 5:6-8)

(Can you imagine dying for your friends? Maybe you can. But would you die for people you don't even know? How about people who hate you and make up lies about you? Would you then? Yeah, right. Exactly.

Not only was Jesus willing to die for his 12 friends, he was willing to die for us. All of us. Everyone. Even those who don't deserve it. Even those who never know him. He loves us that much.)

D. The church started out committed to <u>each</u> <u>other</u>.

"All the believers were one in heart and mind. No one claimed that any of their possessions was their own, but they shared everything they had. With great power the apostles continued to testify to the resurrection of the Lord Jesus. And God's grace was so powerfully at work in them all that there were no needy persons among them. For from time to time those who owned land or houses sold them, brought the money from the sales and put it at the apostles' feet, and it was distributed to anyone who had need." (Acts 4:32-35)

(Most of us can't deal with the thought of sharing our bedroom or even the backseat with our brothers or sisters. But the radical love of Jesus was the bond between this band of brothers.

The love and commitment were so transforming, the church grew out of them. People shared all they had. They cared for each other. They sacrificed for each other. They stood up for one another. They were a band so strong we're here today because of their commitment to and love for each other.)

2. You were <u>created</u> to be part of the Christian band of brothers.

(The Christian band of brothers is so deep and so wide. When you're a follower of Jesus, you're automatically connected with a band of brothers across the world and throughout time. Unfortunately, the church hasn't always been so good at sticking together. However, you were created to change that. You were created to help restore the church to how it was in the beginning.)

"Because we loved you so much, we were delighted to share with you not only the gospel of God but our lives as well." (1 Thessalonians 2:8)

BECOMING A BAND OF BROTHERS

1. Jesus' band of brothers

   A. Who were they? _____ guys. _____ purpose: _____ Jesus.

   "When morning came, he called his disciples to him and chose twelve of them, whom he also designated apostles: Simon (whom he named Peter), his brother Andrew, James, John, Philip, Bartholomew, Matthew, Thomas, James son of Alphaeus, Simon who was called the Zealot, Judas son of James, and Judas Iscariot, who became a traitor." (Luke 6:13-18)

   B. They were committed to _____.

   "Peter replied, 'Even if all fall away on account of you, I never will.' 'Truly I tell you,' Jesus answered, 'this very night, before the rooster crows, you will disown me three times.' But Peter declared, 'Even if I have to die with you, I will never disown you.' And all the other disciples said the same." (Matthew 26:33-35)

   C. He was committed to _____.

   "You see, at just the right time, when we were still powerless, Christ died for the ungodly. Very rarely will anyone die for a righteous person, though for a good person someone might possibly dare to die. But God demonstrates his own love for us in this: While we were still sinners, Christ died for us." (Romans 5:6-8)

   D. The church started out committed to _____.

   "All the believers were one in heart and mind. No one claimed that any of their possessions was their own, but they shared everything they had. With great power the apostles continued to testify to the resurrection of the Lord Jesus. And God's grace was so powerfully at work in them all that there were no needy persons among them. For from time to time those who owned land or houses sold them, brought the money from the sales and put it at the apostles' feet, and it was distributed to anyone who had need." (Acts 4:32-35)

2. You were _____ to be part of the Christian band of brothers.

   "Because we loved you so much, we were delighted to share with you not only the gospel of God but our lives as well." (1 Thessalonians 2:8)

MATCH THE BANDS

A band of brothers isn't simply a group of guys who get together. Bands of brothers are known for their love for and commitment to each other.

Having a band of brothers isn't something new. There are and have been all sorts of "bands" who've met together throughout history.

Match the bands of brothers' descriptions on the left with the bands' names on the right.

1. These guys go to the same university and live in a house together.

2. These men are committed to growing in their faith and keeping each other accountable.

3. These guys fight the heat together.

4. These brothers play in a band together.

5. These guys followed Jesus.

6. These guys rescued the princess.

7. These men are bound by crime fighting.

8. These guys have fought battles together.

9. These dudes meet every week with the best youth leader ever: _____.

10. These guys are all for one and one for all. And they have a great candy bar.

Band Names

A. Police officers

B. Three Musketeers

C. US!

D. Veterans

E. Van Halen

F. Accountability groups

G. Firefighters

H. Fraternity brothers

I. The disciples

J. Mario Brothers

JOHN WESLEY'S "BAND OF BROTHERS"

On Christmas Day, 1738, John Wesley, the founder of the United Methodist Church, drew up some rules for his bands of brothers. In those days the groups were referred to as "Wesley's bands" or "Wesley's societies." His bands were basically very committed accountability groups.

Wesley was really into creating methods, thus the name of his church: the Methodist Church. He was so intense about the commitment level of each band, you couldn't just join it. You had to pass an interview.

1. A. He had six rules for each band:

   ▷ Meet once a week.

   ▷ Start on time.

   ▷ Begin with prayer or singing.

   ▷ Everyone share the sin(s) they've struggled with that week.

   ▷ Pray for each other at the end of meeting time.

   ▷ Have one person lead each meeting by sharing from his own life first.

   B. Each man answered at least the following four questions:

   ▷ What known sins have you committed since our last meeting?

   ▷ How have you been tempted this week?

   ▷ How did you fight that temptation?

   ▷ What have you thought, said, or done that you're not sure whether it's sinful or not?

Wesley was serious about wanting to live a holy life and honoring God. He knew he couldn't do it alone.

2. If you were to create your own band of brothers based on encouraging, helping, and keeping each other accountable, what would be some of your rules?

3. If you were to create three questions each member of your band had to answer every time you met, what would they be?

   A.

   B.

   C.

SOUL WORK

In the national bestseller *Real Boys' Voices*[9], William S. Pollack shares a number of stories written by guys from all over the country. Here's one:

> I can talk to my dad about any problems at school. He's a really good listener. I would imagine I'm a good listener, too, but only when I want to be a good listener. When something interests me, I listen very well. My friends come to me with their problems sometimes, and they tell me things about their girlfriends and what's going on with them.
>
> I look up to my dad. I sometimes go on bike rides with him, and sometimes he helps with my homework. We mostly do family things. I think he works really, really hard, and I think he's a great man. He has a good way of dealing with people. He's smart, and he has an excellent sense of humor. I think that's what I admire most about him. When I grow up, I'd like to be a combination of a great actor and a person with my dad's personality. I really like him.

What are five things you like most about your dad or stepdad? If you don't have a dad, write the five things you like most about the man you look up to most.

1. _____
2. _____
3. _____
4. _____
5. _____

Tell him what you wrote and have him sign his autograph in the box. If you can't, take some time to thank God for being your heavenly Father.

> I love you, Dad.

[9] Pollack, William S. Real Boys' Voices. New York: Penguin Books, 2000.

CHAPTER EIGHT

FATHER HUNGER: GETTING TO KNOW YOUR HEAVENLY DAD

THE BIG IDEA

Nurture your relationship with the perfect Father.

Main Text

> "Take delight in the LORD and he will give you the desires of your heart." (Psalm 37:4)

What's the Point?

No earthly dad is perfect. We can only count on one Father. We'll encourage students to thank God for the dads they have and to seek their fathers' blessing on becoming men who belong more to our heavenly Father than to their earthly ones.

RECAP SOUL WORK

The **Soul Work** for last week had your guys read a great note by a teenager about his dad and then had them talk with their own dads. Some of your guys don't have dads or their dads are unavailable, which probably made this assignment more difficult than usual.

Have your guys share what they talked about and wrote. Then move into your last session with, **Today we're going to talk a lot about dads—especially about developing a relationship with our heavenly Father.**

OPENING ACTIVITY
Option One: Best Dad Stories

Begin your session by having your guys share some of their best stories about their dads. These can be funny stories, sad stories, hero stories, embarrassing stories, or whatever.

Start them off with a story of your own. If you have one, share a funny story about your dad while you were growing up. It'll break the ice, get your guys laughing, be fun, and get you started on the right foot.

When everyone is done sharing, transition to the **Big Picture** by saying something like, **As you can see, no dad is perfect. Some dads try really hard. Other dads just aren't around. And as we'll see, in the Bible even some of the greatest heroes weren't perfect dads.**

Then have the student who most recently celebrated his birthday start you guys off in prayer.

Option Two: Questions about Dads

As we begin this session on dads, prime the pump for the guys by asking them some questions about dads:

▷ **When I say "Dad," what's the first word you think of?**

▷ **If you could have any dad from a television show as your dad, who would you want?**

▷ **How would you describe the perfect dad?**

▷ **What do you admire most about your dad?**

▷ **What's the funniest story you have about your dad?**

▷ **If you could change one thing about your dad, what would it be?**

▷ **What kind of dad do you want to become?**

▷ **What do you think the hardest part about being a dad is?**

When everyone is done sharing, transition to the **Big Picture** by saying something like, **You know, no dad is perfect. Some dads try really hard. Other dads just aren't around. And as we'll see, in the Bible even some of the greatest heroes weren't perfect dads.**

YOU'LL NEED

A bell or a whistle, a tie, a briefcase, a golf club, a cell phone, and pretty much any prop you can think of related to students and dads talking; food, drinks, your guys' dads and their affirmations; enough paper for each of your guys (any type of plain paper will work); tape and pens or markers

Then have the student who most recently celebrated his birthday start you guys off in prayer.

Option Three: Improv Skits—Fathers

Get your guys focusing on dads and laughing with some improv skits. Ask for a couple of sets of volunteers and tell them they'll be doing improv—making up skits—about fathers and sons.

Have two actors step up to the front and pick some of the dad props to use. Then have the rest of your guys give you suggestions of different scenarios for your volunteers to act out. The situations can be anything. If your audience is having trouble thinking of ideas, here's a list to get you started:

▷ Your dad finds the report card you've been hiding.

▷ You and Dad are changing the oil in the family car.

▷ You and Dad are watching a baseball game, and your team hits the winning home run.

▷ You and Dad are fixing a flat tire on the side of a busy road.

▷ Your dad gets pulled over for speeding while teaching you how to drive.

Explain that once they have their scene, you'll get them started by saying, **And...ACTION!** When they're done or you think they've reached their full potential, use the whistle or bell to signify the end of the sketch.

After your newfound Tony Award winners are done, transition to the **Big Picture** by saying something like, **You know, no dad is perfect. Some dads try really hard. Other dads just aren't around. And as we'll see, in the Bible even some of the greatest heroes weren't perfect dads.**

Then have the student who most recently celebrated his birthday start you guys off in prayer.

THE BIG PICTURE

No one teaches a son about what it means to be a man more than his father. Unfortunately, many dads feel unequipped as men themselves or are unavailable, abusive, or deceased.

Our **Outline** session has two parts: First you'll focus on four dads from the Bible and their problems (Noah's drunkenness, Abraham's unavailability, Saul's abusiveness, and Joseph's death).

Next you'll encourage students to trust God as their Father as you demonstrate how Jesus, though his earthly father had likely died, found his identity, worth, and manhood in his relationship with our heavenly Father. Then transition to the **Breakdown**.

BREAKDOWN

Option One: Twenty Fun Ways to Hang Out with Our Heavenly Father

It's one thing to tell your guys to hang out with God. What does that mean, anyway? To some extent they must be wondering.

Help them realize some practical ways to build a relationship and spend time with God by saying something like, **It may sound strange to hear, "Hang out with God." So let me give you 20 fun ways you can hang out with God.**

Pass out the **Twenty Fun Ways to Hang Out with Our Heavenly Father** handout and read a few of the ideas. Have your guys read the rest of them later and move to the **Closing Activity.**

Option Two: Case Studies

Now that you've challenged your guys to look to our heavenly Father as the perfect model of a dad and to seek their worth from him, help them think through what that means with this next option.

Read some or all of the following case studies to your guys and have them offer their best advice. Help them think through what's going on in each situation and apply what you previously taught.

1. **Mike's dad loves sports. Maybe even a bit too much. His dad is really great when Mike comes through with a good play. He's his loudest encourager. Unfortunately, the opposite is**

true whenever Mike makes a mistake. Mike feels so much pressure from his dad to excel in sports, he's beginning to hate sports. What advice can you give him?

2. Joel loves his dad. He has so many great memories of building things together and going to fun events. Unfortunately, his dad has to work the second shift now, so the only time Joel sees his dad is on the weekends. He knows his family needs the money, but he really wishes he could talk to his dad and see him more. What would you say to Joel?

3. Kirk doesn't talk much about his dad. It's been two years since his dad died of a heart attack. He was only 42 years old. So Kirk and his brother and sister are left with a mom who works a lot just to take care of everyone. No one knows, but Kirk is angry at God for taking his dad away from him. How can Kirk find help?

4. Rob's dad doesn't seem like the kind of guy who would hurt his 13-year-old son, but it's happened. More than once this week Rob talked back to his mom, and the last time his dad got up, pushed him, and punched him. Rob didn't talk to his dad for three days. He loves his dad, but he feels his dad was out of line. How can Rob love a dad who would hit him?

Once your guys have rattled off all of their best advice, move to the **Closing Activity** by saying, **Learning to look to God as our Father can be difficult since we can't see God or touch God. However, God's love is the only thing that will ever satisfy us as real men.**

Option Three: "The Empty Chair"[10]

Help your guys understand the grace and peace from having a personal and intimate relationship with God by sharing the following illustration:

> **Author Brennan Manning tells the following story of an old man who was dying of cancer.**
>
> **The man's daughter had asked the local priest to come and pray with her father. When the priest arrived, he found the man lying in bed with his head propped up on two pillows and**

[10] From *Abba's Child* by Brennan Manning. Colorado Springs: NavPress, 1994.

an empty chair beside his bed. The priest assumed the old fellow had been informed of his visit. "I guess you were expecting me," he said.

"No, who are you?"

"I'm the new associate at your parish," the priest replied. "When I saw the empty chair, I figured you knew I was going to show up."

"Oh yeah, the chair," said the bedridden man. "Would you mind closing the door?"

Puzzled, the priest shut the door.

"I've never told anyone this, not even my daughter," said the man. "But all of my life I've never known how to pray. At the Sunday Mass I used to hear the priest talk about prayer, but it always went right over my head.

"I abandoned any attempt at prayer," the old man continued, "until one day about four years ago my best friend said to me, 'Joe, prayer is just a simple matter of having a conversation with Jesus. Here's what I suggest. Sit down on a chair, place an empty chair in front of you, and in faith see Jesus on the chair. It's not spooky because he promised, "I'll be with you always." Then just speak to him and listen in the same way you're doing with me right now.'

"So, Father, I tried it, and I've liked it so much I do it for a couple of hours every day. I'm careful, though. If my daughter saw me talking to an empty chair, she'd either have a nervous breakdown or send me off to the funny farm."

The priest was deeply moved by the story and encouraged the old guy to continue on the journey. Then he prayed with him, anointed him with oil, and returned to the rectory [house where a priest lives].

Two nights later the daughter called to tell the priest her dad had died that afternoon.

"Did he seem to die in peace?" he asked.

"Yes, when I left the house around two o'clock, he called me over to his bedside, told me one of his corny jokes, and kissed me on the cheek. When I got back from the store an hour later, I found him dead. But there was something strange, Father. In fact, beyond strange—kinda weird. Apparently, just before Dad died, he leaned over and rested his head on a chair beside the bed."

Where to take it from here...say, **John, who was known as the beloved disciple, writes twice in his Gospel of the time he leaned against Jesus in a moment of intimacy (John 13:23, 25 and 21:20). It was a special memory for John, assuring him he was indeed a "disciple whom Jesus loved."**

Then say, **Do you have the kind of relationship with Jesus that John did? Are you and Jesus so close you can converse with him as you would with a friend? Do you know he loves you passionately, is interested in you, and wants to listen to everything you have to say? Can you lean against him and feel his heartbeat?**

Move to the **Closing Activity** by saying, **That's the kind of relationship Jesus wants to have with you.**

CLOSING ACTIVITY
Option One: Rite-of-Passage Ceremony

Last week you mailed out letters to your students' dads to have them come for part of this session. Invite the dads into your room now and share with your guys what's about to happen with the rite of passage. Share about how many cultures have rites of passage for their children to go through before they're considered adults. After you're done explaining, have one of the dads begin.

When the last dad is done, close your time together by reading Psalm 37:4 together (it's on the bottom of the Outline). Then have a special time of prayer for your guys and send them off as young men.

Done well, this ceremony will be something the guys remember for a long, long time.

Option Two: Manhood Affirmations

If it doesn't work out to have the rite-of-passage ceremony, you can still have a special time of affirming each of your boys and talking about how they've grown.

Hand each guy a piece of paper and have him put his name at the top. Then have them pass their sheets to the guy to their left, with this instruction: *The guy who just got the sheet writes an affirmation—something real and affirming—(and can sign his name or not) at the BOTTOM of the page, then folds the edge up, covering his note. The next guy writes above that and folds again, etc. Then no one reads what you've written except the intended kid.*

You might say, **By *real* I mean something other than "You're cool." And by affirming I mean something other than "You're cool" or "You don't stink as bad as you used to."**

Finally, take some time yourself to write something to each one of your guys. Have the guys take the pages home at the end of the session. Remember, they'll take these home and maybe keep them for years—who knows how many times they'll read the words you write on these pages?

When your guys are all done, close your time by reading Psalm 37:4 together (it's on the bottom of your **Outline**), have a special time of prayer for your guys, and send them off as young men.

Option Three: Letter from Your Heavenly Father[11]

After spending your session talking about having a relationship with our heavenly Father, wouldn't it be nice for the guys to hear from God? You can give the guys a letter composed of God's words taken from the Bible.

Write letters to your guys made up of different Scriptures. You can paraphrase the passages to make them flow into complete sentences. Be careful not to choose verses you'd have to take way out of context.

---

[11] Fields, Doug, and Duffy Robbins. *Memory Makers*. Grand Rapids, MI: Zondervan, 1996.

Pick some of your favorite verses, ones that mean a lot to you, and personalize the letters for each of your guys. Done well, this letter will become a special keepsake a kid will return to again and again. If you're short on time the week before your meeting, copy and pass out the **Letter from Your Heavenly Father** handout provided.

After you've given out the letters, close your time by reading Psalm 37:4 together (it's on the bottom of your **Outline**), have a special time of prayer for your guys, and send them off as young men.

OUTLINE (LEADER GUIDE)

FATHER HUNGER: GETTING TO KNOW YOUR DAD

1. Famous dads in the Bible

   (There are all sorts of dads in the Bible. Some of them I think will surprise you. Let's start with Noah.)

   A. Noah got <u>drunk</u> and naked.

   "Noah, a man of the soil, proceeded to plant a vineyard. When he drank some of its wine, he became drunk and lay uncovered inside his tent." (Genesis 9:20-21)

   (Yes, this is the same guy who built a giant boat. He isn't known as a drunk, but he did have a bit too much wine one day.)

   B. Abraham *ditched* his first son.

   "Early the next morning Abraham took some food and a skin of water and gave them to Hagar. He set them on her shoulders and then sent her off with the boy. She went on her way and wandered in the Desert of Beersheba." (Genesis 21:14)

   (To make a long story short, Abraham's wife, Sarah, never liked his first son or the other woman he had his son with, Hagar—even though Sarah had told Abraham to have the baby with Hagar! After Sarah's baby was born, she told Abraham to get rid of his first son and his mom. And he did. "See ya, kid. Better luck next time.")

   C. Saul loved his son nearly to <u>death</u>.

   "Saul's anger flared up at Jonathan and he said to him, 'You son of a perverse and rebellious woman!'...Saul hurled his spear at him to kill him." (1 Samuel 20:30, 33)

   (Saul had some real anger-management issues. It didn't take very much to get him unhappy, even to the point of trying to kill his own son.)

   D. Joseph was <u>human</u>.

   (Jesus' earthly father, Joseph, isn't written about very much after Jesus becomes a man, and he's definitely not around when Jesus needs him the most. While some believe Joseph

later left the family, doubting his role as a father and Jesus as the Savior, most assume Joseph died during Jesus' childhood.)

2. So...what do you do when your dad has moments when he shows he isn't perfect?

<u>Hang out</u> with the dad who is.

"Be perfect, therefore, as your heavenly Father is perfect." (Matthew 5:48)

(Even though your dad isn't perfect, one dad is. The same dad Jesus built a relationship with is the same dad you can have a relationship with, too. Jesus was a real man because of his love for the Father. Check it out.)

A. Jesus spent time as an <u>adolescent</u> with our heavenly Father.

"When his parents saw him, they were astonished. His mother said to him, 'Son, why have you treated us like this? Your father and I have been anxiously searching for you.' 'Why were you searching for me?' he asked. 'Didn't you know I had to be in my Father's house?'" (Luke 2:48-49)

B. God was <u>proud</u> of his Son.

"As soon as Jesus was baptized, he went up out of the water. At that moment heaven was opened, and he saw the Spirit of God descending like a dove and alighting on him. And a voice from heaven said, 'This is my Son, whom I love; with him I am well pleased.'" (Matthew 3:16-17)

C. Jesus lived as an adult <u>connected</u> to the Father.

"Very early in the morning, while it was still dark, Jesus got up, left the house and went off to a solitary place, where he prayed." (Mark 1:35)

(Jesus found his identity, his manhood, his worth, and his reason for living in his heavenly Father. You can trust God, too, never to leave you, never to stop loving you, and to never stop helping you become a real man.)

"Take delight in the LORD and he will give you the desires of your heart." (Psalm 37:4)

OUTLINE

FATHER HUNGER: GETTING TO KNOW YOUR DAD

1. Famous dads in the Bible

   A. Noah got d_____ and naked.

   "Noah, a man of the soil, proceeded to plant a vineyard. When he drank some of its wine, he became drunk and lay uncovered inside his tent." (Genesis 9:20-21)

   B. Abraham d_____ his first son.

   "Early the next morning Abraham took some food and a skin of water and gave them to Hagar. He set them on her shoulders and then sent her off with the boy. She went on her way and wandered in the Desert of Beersheba." (Genesis 21:14)

   C. Saul loved his son nearly to d_____.

   "Saul's anger flared up at Jonathan and he said to him, 'You son of a perverse and rebellious woman!'...Saul hurled his spear at him to kill him." (1 Samuel 20:30, 33)

   D. Joseph was h_____.

2. So...what do you do when your dad has moments when he shows he isn't perfect?

   H_____ with the dad who is.

   "Be perfect, therefore, as your heavenly Father is perfect." (Matthew 5:48)

   A. Jesus spent time as an _____ with our heavenly Father.

   "When his parents saw him, they were astonished. His mother said to him, 'Son, why have you treated us like this? Your father and I have been anxiously searching for you.' 'Why were you searching for me?' he asked. 'Didn't you know I had to be in my Father's house?'" (Luke 2:48-49)

B. God was _____ of his Son.

"As soon as Jesus was baptized, he went up out of the water. At that moment heaven was opened, and he saw the Spirit of God descending like a dove and alighting on him. And a voice from heaven said, 'This is my Son, whom I love; with him I am well pleased.'" (Matthew 3:16-17)

C. Jesus lived as an adult _____ to the Father.

"Very early in the morning, while it was still dark, Jesus got up, left the house and went off to a solitary place, where he prayed." (Mark 1:35)

"Take delight in the LORD and he will give you the desires of your heart." (Psalm 37:4)

TWENTY FUN WAYS TO HANG OUT WITH OUR HEAVENLY FATHER

1. Learn to be still and listen for God's voice.

2. Write out your prayers in a journal.

3. Start a new ministry at your church.

4. Ask your parents to buy you a Bible version you'll actually read.

5. Make sure you read the Bible version your parents buy you. Start small.

6. Tell God how great you think he is and why.

7. Listen for God's voice as if you're listening to a conversation between ants (the bugs, not your relatives).

8. Memorize John 3:16.

9. Draw a picture of you and Jesus.

10. Sing a song to God.

11. Confess your sins to God and hear him say, "I love you, and I forgive you."

12. Read one chapter of the book of Proverbs every day. In a month you'll have finished the book.

13. Draw a vertical (up and down) line on a piece of paper. On the left side write your prayer requests ("Help me hear your voice"), and on the right side write down when God answers your prayer and how ("May 5, I heard God's voice for the first time. He said, 'Are you sure you want to do that?'").

14. Repeat this prayer over and over silently for five minutes: "Lord, Jesus Christ, have mercy on me, a sinner." Think about the words you're praying and let them sink in.

15. Go on a walk and thank God for all the amazing things he's created.

16. Be a greeter for your worship service.

17. How about going to church and actually taking notes during the sermon?

18. After you turn off the alarm and before you get out of bed, ask God, "What do you want to teach me today?"

19. Ask your youth leader to recommend a good devotional book to read. (Devotional books are about God and living your life to honor God. There are lots of really good ones.)

20. Find worship music you can download on your iPod and spend time listening and being in God's presence.

LETTER FROM YOUR HEAVENLY FATHER

Dear Son,

I have created you. I've called you by name. You are precious in my sight, and I rejoice over you. In fact, I called you into fellowship with my son, Jesus.

I taught you how to walk in my ways, though you may not have realized it. So seek me day by day, and delight to know my ways. Acknowledge me, and I will respond to you as surely as the coming of the dawn or the rain of early spring.

Come and behold my beauty, Son. Pour out your heart to me like water, and know the refreshment that comes from my presence.

Love always,

Your heavenly Father

(The text of this letter is directly from God's Word. Here's where you can find the verses, in the order they appear above: Isaiah 43:1, Isaiah 43:4, Zephaniah 3:17, 1 Corinthians 1:9, Hosea 11:3, Isaiah 58:2, Hosea 6:3, Psalm 27:4, Lamentations 2:19, and Acts 3:19.)